Saved By Faithfulness

Saved By Faithfulness

How The Covenant Shapes Our
Understanding of Salvation

Mark Skillin

Saved By Faithfulness
Copyright © 2009 by Mark Skillin

Published by
Christ Covenant Church
863 High Street.
Fall River, MA. 02720
www.covenantofchrist.org

ISBN 978-0-615-32495-1

Cover design: Chris Yokel. Photo by Roomic Cube, and is used under the Creative Commons Attribution 2.0 Generic license.

Printed in the United States of America.

Acknowledgements

This book could not have gotten off the ground in its present form without the effort of a team of people who have volunteered their time and talents for the benefit of this project. I am grateful to Mick Yokel and his son Chris for their efforts in formatting and editing, to my father-in-law Doug Hlousek, who meticulously reviewed the manuscript and offered many helpful corrections and suggestions, and to my son Jacob who was involved in the formatting process offering his technical expertise. I am especially grateful to the Lord Jesus Christ, who enabled us to persevere and complete this project five years or so after pen first touched paper. We welcome any comments and suggestions via our church website that would improve the quality of this book. We recognize that flaws may still exist that have escaped our notice.

Table of Contents

Introduction   1

1. Our Covenantal Relationship with the Lord   5

2. God's Covenantal Relationship with Adam and Eve   7

3. The Lord God's Covenant with Abraham   11

4. The Lord's Covenant with Abraham Confirmed   15

5. Abraham's Great Sacrifice by Faith   19

6. The Lord God's Covenant with Israel   25

7. The Lord God, Israel, and the Great Divorce   31

8. Jesus Christ and the Return of the Covenant Lord   37

9. Jesus Christ and His New Covenant   43

10. Paul the Apostle of the New Covenant   51

11. The Lord God's Covenant is To Be Obeyed by Faith   59

12. The Great Divorce Revisited   65

13. The Gospel: Saved by Faithfulness to Christ Alone   71

14. How We Are Justified by the Blood of Jesus   83

15. How We Are Sanctified by the Blood of Jesus   89

16. The Apostle Paul: Pressing on to the Goal of Eternal Life   95

17. Where Do We Go from Here?   99

18. The Covenantal Lens   105

Appendix: Storming the Strong Towers of Faith Alone   113

Introduction

There is nothing more important to mankind than the good news of Jesus Christ our Lord. Life and death hang in the balance; not just life and death as understood on this earth, but life and death as an everlasting experience of every human being. This is not a subject with which we can afford to be shallow and thoughtless. The good news of Jesus Christ must be understood in the way the Scriptures themselves present this message. The good news of God's salvation must be embraced for what it is in its entirety, devoid of the "human ballast" that so grieved Dietrich Bonhoeffer a generation ago.[1] Our present day struggle is to continue the Reformation. We must reform; but we must reform according to the Scriptures of our Lord. Martin Luther will not be our judge. How the church "stands or falls" is not according to his word, but according to the revealed will of God. The Reformation was the result of hard work and deep thought, which is precisely what we need today. The church is becoming increasingly shallow, trivial and thoughtless. We must resist these tendencies and fight hard to hear God again through His holy Word.

This book is the fruit of hard fought efforts to hear God's Word as it is meant to be heard. His Word is not meant as material for our entertainment, nor is it a servant of our doctrinal traditions. God's Word is deadly serious, and is seriously committed to the glory of the one true God. God's Word is the keeper of God's traditions, the traditions of the apostles. It is God's Word which will judge all traditions, be they Catholic, Greek Orthodox, Protestant, Reformed or Emergent. People who love God more than anything else will delight in nothing less than the holy will of our Lord as revealed in Scripture. People who love God will also delight in the teachings of men, but only as these men fight hard to hear God's Word as it is meant to be heard. We strive to hear from God because we want the life He offers us in Scripture. We don't

---

1   Dietrich Bonhoeffer, *The Cost of Discipleship.* Simon & Schuster, 1959, 35. "The real trouble is that the pure Word of Jesus has been overlaid with so much human ballast – burdensome rules and regulations, false hopes and consolations – that it becomes extremely difficult to make a genuine decision for Christ."

1

want any substitutes, no matter how popular they may be, nor how long they may have been believed.

Our God is a God who has committed Himself to His people. He has tangibly expressed His commitment through the means of covenants. In the Old Testament He covenanted with Adam, Noah, Abraham, and Israel; now in the New Testament He has given us a New Covenant. In fact, "testament" is derived from the Latin word for covenant, so our Scriptures are actually divided into two covenants, the Old and the New. To have a relationship with God is to be in covenant with God. Therefore, it is imperative that we listen closely to God's Word in order to understand what it means for us to be in a covenantal relationship with Him. I am grateful to be living in our times when so much progress has been made toward a more biblical understanding of this covenantal relationship, and I am also grateful to those who have not rested contentedly with discoveries of the past, but have pressed on in the spirit of the reformers who have gone before, looking intently into the "royal law found in Scripture" (Jas. 2:8). This pressing on toward a better understanding is not being disobedient to the intent of the apostles; rather it is commanded by them. It was Peter who exhorted the church to "grow in the grace and the knowledge of our and Savior Lord Jesus Christ" (2 Pet. 2:17). In some small way, may this work continue what Dr. C. van der Waal could not finish when he wrote, "It is impossible to preach a gospel from which the covenant has been removed. It is impossible to speak of the kingship of God, without bringing the covenant into it. The Great King is the God of the covenant. His royal Word is covenantal."[2]

I present this book to all who are led by our Lord to inquire about the nature of the covenant that He has made with his people. I am especially grateful to so many who have helped me in my own inquiry through their studies and writings; Meredith Kline, Norman Shepherd, Scott Hafemann, NT Wright, William Law, Dietrich Bonhoeffer, C. Van der Waal, Jonathan Edwards, Richard Gaffin and Daniel Fuller among others. They have helped me in various ways to think more biblically about the covenant. But I am most grateful to the apostle James, who grabbed me by the scruff of the neck and wouldn't let me go, by writing, "You see, a man is justified by works and not by faith alone." This sentence pricked and prodded me to question my own evangelical tradition, as every time I read it, it became more incredible to me that

---

2   C van der Waal, *The Covenantal Gospel*. Inheritance Publications, 1990, 175.

the brother of Jesus and pastor of the church in Jerusalem would make, what has become for many, an unorthodox statement in defense of orthodoxy. James has not inspired me toward Roman Catholicism, as it may be presumed by many, but he has inspired me to become more biblical in my understanding of how the covenant functions, and in being more biblical, to become more evangelical. The purpose of writing this book is to help others to understand what I have come to understand concerning God's covenant and the salvation it promises. My own conviction is that this is the great need of our day. The church faces many potent challenges and we need the covenant as a safeguard against worldliness and apostasy. This is true, because as the Scriptures reveal, it is the covenant that pledges us to our Lord, and it is the covenant that motivates us to "throw off everything that hinders and the sin that so easily entangles." My hope and prayer is that God is glorified by this small, and by his grace alone, faithful explanation of His covenant.

Pastor Mark C. Skillin M.Div. Th.M.
Christ Covenant Church
Fall River, Massachusetts

1.

Our Covenantal Relationship with the Lord

It is virtually beyond dispute that our relationship with God is covenantal. Most theological schools of thought agree on at least this basic point. The two major periods that characterize this biblical history are in fact covenantal: the period of the Old Covenant, followed by the New Covenant and our Bibles are divided into two sections reflecting these two major periods of covenantal history. In fact, what we have typically called the Old Testament and the New Testament would more accurately be titled the Old Covenant and the New Covenant since the English word "testament" is derived from the Latin *testamentum*, which means "covenant". So the Old Testament and New Testament writings are understood to be expressions of the two main covenants that God has made with His people.

God Himself characterizes His relationship with mankind as being covenantal in character. We read of God's understanding of His relationship with man as being covenantal in Genesis 6:18 when He said to Noah, "But I will establish my *covenant*[3] with you, and you will enter the ark - you and your sons and your wife and your son's wives with you." In Psalm 25:14, David rejoices in the reality that "The Lord confides in those who fear him; he makes his *covenant* known to them." Isaiah proclaims the problem of mankind in Isaiah 24:5, "The earth is defiled by its people; they have disobeyed the laws, violated the statutes and broken the everlasting *covenant*." This passage shows all mankind to be in a covenantal relationship with God. Hosea indicts Israel for the same unfaithfulness that characterizes all mankind when he announces, "Put the trumpet to the lips! An eagle is over the house of the Lord because my people have broken my *covenant* and rebelled against my law" (Hos. 8:1).

Jeremiah as well speaks of this "broken covenant," and at the

---

3   Italics are added to Scriptural quotations throughout for emphasis.

same time prophecies of a day when God will make a "New Covenant" with His people. "'The time is coming,' declares the Lord, 'when I will make a *New Covenant* with the house of Israel and with the house of Judah. It will not be like the *covenant* I made with their forefathers when I took them by the hand to lead them out of Egypt, because they broke my *covenant*, though I was a husband to them,' declares the Lord" (Jer. 31:31, 32).

It was this change in covenantal relationship from the Old to the New that the writer of Hebrews describes as being in process in his day, "By calling this *covenant* 'new,' he made the first one obsolete; and what is obsolete and aging will soon disappear" (Heb. 8:13). The Apostle Paul also understood the apostolic ministry to be covenantal in nature, as he describes himself and his fellow apostles as ministers of the New Covenant. "He has made us competent as ministers of a New Covenant - not of the letter but of the Spirit; for the letter kills, but the Spirit gives life" (2 Co. 3:6). So it should be clear from these passages that our relationship with our Lord is covenantal, no matter what period of redemptive history you live in. This is explicitly stated from the time of Noah to the Apostle Paul, and it seems clear that this is a fact that our Lord wants us to understand.

But the question remains: how does this fact shed light on our relationship to Him? Now we must take a closer look at the content of our covenantal relationship with God. The best way to approach this is to examine chronologically from Adam to Jesus Christ the covenantal way in which God has related to His people. Through God's covenants with Adam, Abraham, Moses and Jesus, a full understanding of this covenantal relationship can be discerned. This approach follows the logic of the Bible, as the Bible itself is an unfolding historical account of God's relationship with His people.

2.

God's Covenantal Relationship with Adam and Eve

In Genesis 1 we read of God's power and wisdom in the creation of the heavens and the earth. God stands at the center of this account as the One from whom all things come. The grandeur of God's creative activity had been revealed to Moses. The account is marked by God's ringing affirmation of His creation as not just good, but "very good" (Gen. 1:31). The culmination of the creation account is found in Genesis 2:1,2, where God is depicted as resting from His work. The creation is complete.

Genesis 2 then repeats the creation account, from the perspective of God's relationship to Adam. The emphasis of Genesis 2 is a relational one, or in other words, a covenantal one. This is seen first in how God is now referred to as "the Lord God." God is not just the creator, but now He is understood to be the Master, and He is the Lord or Master of Adam. But what kind of Lord is He? The writer of this chapter takes great pains to report that the Lord is a supremely gracious Master. He has provided Adam with everything he could ever need, with trees that were "pleasing to the eye and good for food" (Gen. 2:9). In fact, Adam was told by this gracious Lord that he was "free to eat from any tree in the garden," except for one (Gen. 2:16). The Lord also made Adam a lord over the earth, with the responsibility to oversee the beasts of the earth. The Master provided Adam with abundant provision from His world, but also a great responsibility to care for and oversee His world.

The Lord's generosity and provision culminated in the great blessing of a "helper," Eve, who was perfectly designed for Adam. The Lord God is revealed to be an eminently generous and gracious Master indeed. These are the privileges that God blessed Adam with. In Genesis 2, there is never a hint of there being any lack in Adam's

7

existence, therefore there was nothing Adam needed. In this regard, even the Tree of Life was not off limits. It is explicitly noted that there were two trees in the middle of the garden, but only one was deemed off limits, the tree of the knowledge of good and evil.

So, Adam's relationship with his Lord was characterized by privileges and obligations. He was obligated both positively and negatively. Positively, he was obligated to care for and oversee creation itself, he was to be lord of God's world. Negatively, Adam was obligated to *not* do something. It was the existence of the tree of the knowledge of good and evil that provided Adam's negative obligation to the Lord God. He was obligated to God to *not* eat of this tree.

Adam was living in the midst of God's blessing and he had nothing to gain in meeting this obligation, because he already had it all. He had the Lord God and His creation forever. However, he did have something to lose if he failed to fulfill his obligations. This is why God's promise to Adam had to do with what he stood to lose and not with anything he stood to gain. God never says, "Obey me in this and I will give you something more." There is no word of a promised blessing, but there is word of a promised curse. "You must not eat from the tree of the knowledge of good and evil, for when you eat of it you will surely die" (Gen. 2:16). Adam needed to believe the Lord God when He spoke, and by believing, obey His command not to eat.

It was at this crucial point of faith in God's revealed Word that the serpent strikes in Genesis 3, like a precision missile used in modern warfare. Precision strikes are designed to hit a target at a key point that will bring the greatest destruction. The serpent challenges Adam's helper, Eve, at precisely the points that would undermine her faith, which would then cause her to disobey the Lord. His interrogation of Eve reveals his intent to undermine Eve's understanding of the Lord's credibility and graciousness. First, the serpent misrepresents what the Lord actually said in order to call into question His graciousness when he asked, "Did God *really* say, 'You must not eat from any tree in the garden'?" (Gen. 3:1). In fact, the Lord did *not* say they could not eat from *any* tree. Actually the reverse was true, they could eat from *every* tree, save one!

Eve corrects the serpent on this point, but like a crafty lawyer who successfully plants seeds of doubt into the minds of the jury, he planted doubt in Eve's mind and the damage was done. The serpent then explicitly attacks God's credibility by countering God's promise of a future curse by a promise of his own, "You will not surely die." The serpent then asserts his own promised blessing that they would eat and their eyes would be opened and they would be "like God, knowing good and evil" (Gen. 3:5). The serpent, in a crafty and deceptive way, calls God a miser and a liar. The serpent depicts the Lord as misrepresenting the truth in order to deprive Adam and Eve of something that would be beneficial to them. Eve believed the serpent and by faith in his word she obeyed him and ate what had been forbidden to her. She failed to believe God's revealed Word to her and through her unbelief she disobeyed the Lord's command.

The tragedy is that she trusted a liar, and on the day she and Adam ate what had been forbidden, something sacred did, in fact, die. Death, defined as separation from God and loss of His creational blessing, was immediate. Pain, fear, grief and shame would enter Adam and Eve's consciousness for the first time, and these emotional plagues would not go away. There was no turning back. The Lord God, contrary to the serpent, is infallibly true to His Word. This immediate spiritual death that the Lord God had promised would find its consummation in physical death, "for dust you are and to dust you will return" (Gen. 3:19b). Adam, who truly had nothing more to gain, believed that he did, and by believing the serpent, he lost everything for himself and mankind.

What we are able to discern in God's relationship to Adam and Eve is a relationship characterized by privileges and obligations. Adam and Eve had the wonderful privilege of a relationship with the Lord God; with all the attendant blessings of His grace, and the enjoyment of the fullness of His creation, which was "very good." They also had the obligation to obey God by faith in God's Word to them. In this relationship we see the covenant.

Adam had not earned this relationship through anything he did; it was freely given to him by God. The Lord was in no way obligated to Adam as a debtor because the blessing of God and His creation was given freely. However, to remain in this blessedness, Adam had to obey the Lord. In other words, Adam's continued experience of the life that he had was conditioned upon obeying God through faith in His Word.

Here we see the first manifestation of the covenant. *If* Adam was to disobey God by not believing God's promised curse, then he would die. But *if he* would obey God by faith in His Word to him, *then* he would continue to live. The Lord God had demonstrated His faithfulness and was continuing to demonstrate it to Adam, and Adam was obligated to remain faithful to the Lord God in return. The relationship was covenantal. But this is just the beginning. What we find is that this covenantal relationship was the essence of God's relationship with Abraham as well.

3.

The Lord God's Covenant with Abraham

We first meet Abram in Genesis 11:26-32. We learn that Abram originally came from Ur in Mesopotamia and was the son of Terah. Abram's father, Terah, decided to move with his family from Ur to Canaan but ended up settling in Haran, which is well short of Canaan. We read in Joshua 24 that "Terah, the father of Abraham and Nahor, lived beyond the river and worshiped other gods" (Josh. 24:2). Then in Joshua 24:3, the Lord states, "But I took your father Abraham from the land beyond the River and led him throughout Canaan." The "land beyond the river" would be Ur in Mesopotamia, on the other side of the Euphrates. So we read that God was sovereignly at work in Abram's life, even while he was a worshiper of idols in Ur.

We first read of an explicit meeting of the Lord and Abram in Genesis 12:1-5. The first recorded words to Abram are a command from God, "Leave your country, your people and your father's household and go to the land I will show you" (Gen. 12:1). Here the Lord orders Abram to do something which would have been very radical and risky in the ancient world, to leave his people and his land. There were no relocation departments, highways, or police to ensure safe and convenient travel. This was a command to step out into the great unknown and much potential danger and away from all known security. The Lord did not present this as one option among others; this was something Abram had to do.

However, the Lord did not command Abram to venture into the unknown, without at the same time, giving him promises to hold onto. In fact, the Lord follows His unequivocal command with wonderful assurances of a blessed, prosperous and happy future in which the Lord Himself would be Abram's shield in the world. In so many words, the Lord promised that whatever blessings Abram was experiencing in

Haran would be multiplied one hundredfold, in land, people and fame. The Lord promised him, "I will make you into a great nation and I will bless you; I will make your name great, and you will be a blessing. I will bless those who bless you, and whoever curses you I will curse; and all peoples on earth will be blessed through you" (Gen. 12:3). It is apparent that Abram took the Lord at His Word, because we read in verse 4, "So Abram left, as the Lord had told him; and Lot went with him."

The Lord graciously provided Abram with wonderful promises in order to enable him to obey what would have been a very difficult command. But Abram had to believe the promises, because if he would not trust the Lord by taking Him at his Word, then he would not have been able to obey God's command to go, because it would have been far too risky. But Abram did believe, and it was his faith in God's promises that enabled him to obey as we read in Hebrews 11:8, "By faith Abraham, when called to go to a place he would later receive as his inheritance, obeyed and went, even though he did not know where he was going."

Here we see once again, a relationship with God that is characterized by privileges and obligations. What was Abram's obligation? What was required of him? It was required of him that he leave his home and family. This was commanded of him. What was the privilege that Abram would enjoy? Wonderful blessings! A happy future that would be more than he could imagine. How was Abram to enjoy these wonderful privileges? By meeting the obligation of obeying the Lord when he spoke.

Here we are able to discern the same covenantal relationship that God had with Adam. The only difference between the two is that Adam had everything to lose in not meeting the obligations, while Abram had everything to gain. The Lord's covenant with Abram was God's gracious covenant on the other side of the fall into sin. Abram was called *out of* idolatry and condemnation by the promises of God's blessing and protection and provision, while Adam fell out of God's blessing and protection and provision. For both, meeting obligations was the key to enjoying the privileges. And for both as well, faith in God's promise to them was key in being able to keep their respective obligations. For Adam, it was a promised curse, "you will surely die," since there was nothing more for Adam to gain. Abram, however, was given promised blessings.

As we saw earlier, Adam and Eve fell because of unbelief. They did not take the Lord God at His Word. And here we see Abram entering into God's blessing by faith. He stepped out of the security of what was known and into obedience by standing on God's promise of a land that he could not see. Though the outcome was much different, the relationship between the Lord and Abram and Adam was the same–it was covenantal. But we are not yet finished with Abram since there is much more to this story.

4.

The Lord's Covenant with Abram is Confirmed

By the time we read the verses of Genesis 15, approximately seven years had passed since the Lord had called Abram out of Haran and much had happened. However, one crucial thing had not happened. Even though seven years prior the Lord had promised He would make Abram into a great nation, he and his wife, Sarai remained childless. Of course, the birth of children is required in order to make Abram's descendants "like the dust of the earth," but Abram had yet to see the birth of his first son.

Also, during this seven year period, Abram was still very much a stranger in a foreign land. He had traveled all the way to Egypt and returned, but had yet to settle into a land of his own that stretched "as far as the eyes can see." Instead, he had settled for a plot of land beneath the trees of Mamre. The reality of Abram's existence far undershot the grand promises of God that led him out of Haran. This evidently caused Abram to be discouraged. We can discern his discouragement when reading of his interaction with the Lord in Genesis 15.

The Lord initiates the conversation by exhorting Abram, "Do not be afraid, Abram. I am your shield, your very great reward" (Gen. 15:1). Abram responded, "'O Sovereign Lord, what can you give me since I remain childless and the one who will inherit my estate is Eliezer of Damascus?' And Abram said, 'You have given me no children; so a servant in my household will be my heir'" (15:2, 3). The Lord's exhortation reveals Abram's uncertainty; he was tempted to give up on the Lord's promise and give way to fear produced by unbelief. It is here in Genesis 15 that the Lord re-states, in graphic and striking ways, the promise he made seven years earlier.

First, he reassures Abram by repeating the promise but with more emphasis on the fact that a child will "come from your own body and be your heir." Earlier, in Genesis 12, the Lord compared the number of Abram's descendants to "the dust of the earth," but now he uses an even more glorious analogy by having Abram look up at the night sky and saying to him, "count the stars - if indeed you can count them" and then the Lord said - "so shall your offspring be" (Gen 15:4, 5). Abram was encouraged and believed the Lord, and his heart was set at peace by the Lord's assurances. We know this because of Genesis 15:6, "He believed the Lord, and he credited it to him as righteousness." Of course. this was not the first time Abram had faith. He also had faith in Genesis 12 and he had trusted the Lord ever since. But here in this encounter, the Lord renewed His commitment to Abram, and Abram's faith was renewed in turn. The Lord and Abram continue in faithfulness to each other.

The Lord then drove the reality of His covenant faithfulness home to Abram by employing a graphic covenant-making ceremony. We use a covenant-making ceremony with today's marriage ceremony. The exchange of rings accompanies vows of faithfulness to one another. The ring ceremony is a symbolic illustration of what is stated verbally. With Abram the Lord does something similar, yet very different. He commanded Abram to prepare a ceremony common in Abram's day. Typically, a king would establish a covenant treaty with a vassal, or a king of a lesser city, by having them agree to certain terms having to do with privileges and obligations toward one another. The vassal, or lesser king, would verbally pledge his loyalty to the greater king in agreement with the terms of the covenant.[4] He would then walk between the carcasses of animals that had been cut in half and spread out on the ground. The sacrificed animals signified the penalty that would befall the lesser king for breaking his pledge of loyalty. Walking through the animals signified recognition of and agreement with the covenantal terms. The covenant was then officially ratified, just like when rings are given in the marriage ceremony, the vow is now symbolically ratified.

This is precisely what we see the Lord do in Genesis 15:9-21. He didn't promise to do any more for Abram than what He had already promised in Genesis 12. What he did was ratify His words with a graphic ceremony of commitment. However, the Lord did the opposite

---

4 O. Palmer Robertson, *The Christ of the Covenants.* P&R, 1980, 129-130.

of what we might expect from Him. Given how this ceremony worked in the ancient world, we would expect Abram, who is the lesser, to be made to walk between the animal halves, swearing allegiance to the greater, the Lord God. But the Lord did the opposite. Rather than Abram walking between the sacrificed animals, the Lord Himself symbolically walked between the sacrifices by sending a vision of a smoking fire-pot with a blazing torch while Abram looked on. The Lord was guaranteeing His fidelity to His promises at the cost of His own life, if necessary! The ceremony was concluded with these words, "On that day the Lord made a covenant with Abram...." This was how Abram "can know that (he) will gain possession of it" (Gen. 15:8). The promise is made *with a ceremonial vow.* The writer of Hebrews explains it this way,

> Men swear by someone greater than themselves, *and the oath confirms what is said* and puts an end to all argument. Because God wanted to *make the unchanging nature of his purpose very clear* to the heirs of what was promised, he confirmed it with an oath. God did this so that, by two unchangeable things by which it is impossible for God to lie, we who have fled to take hold of the hope offered to us may be greatly encouraged (Heb. 6:16-18).

The point of confirming "what is said" by an oath is to encourage those who are tempted to be discouraged with God's promise. This is precisely what the Lord was doing for Abram in his time of need. And it would be the encouragement of the Lord's faithfulness that would enable Abram to remain faithful to the Lord and trust Him. It would be this steadfast faith in the promised privileges that would enable Abram to obey His Lord and keep his obligations.

5.

Abraham's Great Sacrifice by Faith

By the time we come to the verses of Genesis 22, almost forty years had passed from the covenant confirming ceremony of Genesis 15. During that time, much had happened to both test and encourage Abraham's faith, as he experienced the Lord's covenantal faithfulness time and again. Abraham was tested by the threat of being murdered by foreign kings who would desire his wife, yet was encouraged by the Lord's deliverance and blessing of an increased flock and respect from those around him (Gen. 12:10-20; 20:1-18). Again Abraham's faith was tested by the existence of evil nations and the possibility of his nephew being caught up in their judgment. Yet his faith was strengthened in seeing God spare the righteous and destroy the wicked with awe inspiring power (Gen. 19:1-29). Once again Abraham's faith was tested by his impatient wife's strong desire for a child, which would result in disregard for the promise. Again he was strengthened through the God-wrought miraculous birth of Isaac, the child promised so long ago (Gen. 16:1-16; 21:1-6).

God is true to His Word. The Lord who had covenanted with Abraham is an infinitely faithful God and Abraham's life lesson that the Lord "is his shield, his very great reward" was being learned. But nothing that had occurred in the last forty years would compare to the great test Abraham was to endure. What Abraham could not foresee, and we can only know by hindsight, is that all along the Lord was preparing Abraham for his great test of covenant faithfulness. Abraham had seen the Lord's covenant faithfulness over and over again and now it would be time for the Lord to see Abraham's faithfulness to Him. It was time for Abraham to glorify God for the God that He truly is, and to manifest to all the world the faithfulness of the Lord. This was to be done in the only way that it could be done to maximize Abraham's faithfulness to the Lord, and at the very same time display, in the greatest way possible the absolute dependability of the Lord.

The word came to Abraham without fanfare and with stark simplicity, "Take your son, your only son, Isaac, whom you love, and go the region of Moriah. Sacrifice him there as a burnt offering on one of the mountains I will tell you about" (Gen. 22:2). In other words, "Abraham, go kill your son." We are given no descriptions of Abraham's anguish. Abraham simply did what he was told.

The whole account breathes of a powerful faith in action. Abraham had the presence of mind to instruct his son Isaac to help him with the preparations, and Isaac hadn't a clue as to what was about to take place. This was a sign that Abraham, though no doubt a man experiencing internal struggle, was a man boldly intent on doing what he had been told. This was the polar opposite of Jonah, who, in Jonah 1:1, insanely ran away from God's will for him.

Abraham was more like Jesus would be in his third and final year of ministry, heading for crucifixion in Jerusalem. Jesus was a man with internal struggle, no doubt, but you did not want to attempt to prevent Him from doing what he knew He had to do. Peter tried, and would regret it (Mt. 16:22, 23). Jesus was aggressively focused to perform what had to be done. This was how Abraham was in Genesis 22. God's Word had come and there was only one way to respond to God's Word when it came—it had to be done. It is impossible to believe that he would *not* have to plunge a knife into his son and then burn him as a whole burnt offering, because the text refuses us this strategy of downsizing Abraham's faith and correspondingly downsizing the Lord's faithfulness. The narrator is clear. He recorded that Abraham "took the knife to slay his son" (22:10). The Lord had to shout to prevent the slaying of Isaac because Abraham's will was fully engaged to perform the act. Death to the one Abraham loved was imminent and Abraham's faithfulness to the Lord rang through the universe! We stand back in astonishment at what Abraham would be willing to do. Abraham would be willing to do the unthinkable because his faith was in the unshakable faithfulness of the Lord.

In Genesis 22, we do not get insight into Abraham's mind-set as to *how* Abraham would be able to kill his son, but we do in Hebrews 11. It is in Hebrews that we understand Abraham, spoken of in Genesis 22, to be a man of mature and time- tested faith. Abraham knew that the Lord was true to His word because he had experienced His faithfulness many times. God had promised many times, and by covenantal oath, that many descendants would come from the living bodies of Abraham's descendants. So from this understanding, Abraham had reasonably concluded that he would kill his only son, Isaac, and sometime afterward the Lord would raise him from the dead (Heb. 11:19). Isaac would die by stabbing and be burned into oblivion. But Abraham's belief was that God was so powerfully true to His Word, that no matter what was done to Isaac, he would live to bear descendants. Abraham understood Isaac to be invincible, not because there was anything special about Isaac, but that he was invincible because God's Word concerning him was invincible. Abraham believed God, so he was able to obey the unthinkable command. Abraham was faithful to His Lord to the uttermost, and in so being, he proclaimed the Lord to be faithful to the uttermost.

On Mount Moriah there was a festival, a climax of mutual allegiance. Abraham and the Lord shouting to one another in one magnificent and anguished moment - "Yes, I am yours!" "Abraham! Abraham!" "Here I am," he replied. "Do not lay a hand on the boy," he said. "Do not lay a hand on him. Now I know that you fear God, because you have not withheld from me your son, your only son" (Gen. 22:11, 12).

"Now I know," God said. However, we might ask, "But didn't God already know what was in Abraham's heart?" Yes, of course He did. But faith requires a demonstration, it must be seen. It must be shown to the world just like love in the heart must be expressed through word and deed. Our relationships require it. We cannot say we love our wives and then do the opposite of what love requires. It is in the doing that the saying becomes real. This is what James states about Abraham in his letter, "You see that his faith and his actions were working together, and his faith was made complete by what he did" (Jas. 2:22). Faith becomes a justifying faith only when accompanied by action. For James it is not as though you lay actions next to faith, and the two added together save; it is that faith produces actions which in turn render faith to be real.

This is how James can say that it was not faith alone that justified Abraham, but that he was "justified by works," works that establish faith, as saving faith. It is through faith demonstrated that God is glorified as the God that He is; and it is faith demonstrated to the uttermost, to the loss of life if necessary that glorifies the Lord to be

21

faithful to the uttermost. Nothing less than this is true faith.

In Genesis 22, Abraham was shown to be righteous by his supreme action. In Genesis 15, the Lord reckoned his faith as righteousness, because that is what Abram was being exhorted *to do*. To do otherwise in that moment would be to call God a liar as Adam had done previously. Now, in Genesis 22, the Lord reckoned Abraham's obedience to the command as his righteousness, and it is on the basis of his faithful obedience that the Lord guarantees His faithfulness to Abraham:

> The angel of the Lord called to Abraham from heaven a second time and said, "I swear by myself, declares the Lord, that *because you have done this* and have not withheld your son, your only son, I will surely bless you and make your descendants as numerous as the stars in the sky and as the sand on the seashore. Your descendants will take possession of the cities of their enemies, and through your offspring all nations on earth will be blessed, *because you have obeyed me"* (Gen. 22:15-18).

God repeated the promise and it was upheld on the basis of Abraham's obedience. The reason the Lord would deliver on His promise is *because* Abraham had been faithful to the Lord, even to the point of losing his one and only son. This is how James can describe Abraham to be "justified by works and not by faith alone." Abraham was truly justified by what he did. The basis or ground of Abraham's reception of the promise was obedience to a command. It is impossible to believe God and at the same time refuse to do what God commands. *This is true because the Lord does not grant the privileges apart from the keeping of the obligations.* The Lord Himself connects the promised privileges with the necessity of keeping the obligations.

Things could not remain the same with Adam *apart from* Adam's obedience to the Lord. Likewise, Abraham could not expect to receive what was promised *apart from* doing exactly what the Lord told him to do, first in leaving Haran, then in sacrificing his only son. If he could receive what was promised apart from doing what the Lord told him to do, then Abraham's obedience becomes optional. If Abraham could have been justified by faith alone and *apart from* obedience to his Lords' commands, then Abraham's behavior becomes incomprehensible. But we see from Adam's experience that obedience was not optional, and we see from Abraham's bold intention to do what he was told, that he was doing what he considered to be absolutely necessary. No father would do what Abraham was willing to do unless there was no other way.

Here we see all the elements of the covenantal relationship. Abraham, like Adam, had wonderful covenantal privileges from a gracious Lord. At the same time both had covenantal obligations that had to be met. Abraham succeeded where Adam and Eve failed. How was Abraham able to keep the covenantal obligations? The only way possible, by trusting the Lord and taking Him at His Word. How was it that Adam and Eve failed? Adam and Eve failed because they believed the serpent and called God a liar. The Lord God keeps His promises. And because the Lord keeps His promises, Adam and Eve would surely die, but the descendants of Isaac would increase into a great nation indeed.

6.

The Lord God's Covenant with Israel

The Lord had promised Abraham that, through his son Isaac, he would give birth to a great multitude, and so he did. A few generations later, Abraham's descendants would be described as "exceedingly numerous, so that the land was filled with them" (Ex. 1:7). However, the second part of God's promise was yet to be fulfilled. This numerous people were not yet in a land they could call their own. In fact, they would find themselves as a great multitude within another nation, the nation of Egypt. Through Joseph, the Lord had led Isaac's descendants out of famine in Canaan, and into the plentiful land of Egypt. Initially they enjoyed much favor and peace within Egypt, but as time went on the attitude of the Egyptians toward the descendants of Isaac would change. The rapid numerical growth of the Israelites would cause the Egyptians to become anxious. So anxious, in fact, that Pharaoh devised a wicked plan to weaken them, through slavery and the systematic murder of their male infants.

The Lord's promise to Abraham had to be kept, so he sent a deliverer to the Israelites with God's power and authority; Moses. Moses was commissioned to lead Israel out of slavery and death and into the land that the Lord God had promised Abraham over two hundred years earlier. It was after this great and powerful deliverance, in which the Lord demonstrated His might in awe inspiring ways, that the Lord covenanted once again with His people. This time the Lord was not covenanting with two people as with Adam and Eve, nor with a single family as with Abraham, but now He was covenanting with a whole nation - a great multitude. We see this formal covenantal arrangement beginning in Exodus 19 at Mount Sinai. Moses was the messenger of the Lord for Israel, and He called Moses to Himself on the mountain, where He told Moses exactly what he was to say to the people. First, Moses was to remind Israel of the Lord's great faithfulness in delivering Israel out of an impossible situation through profound miraculous power. "You yourselves have seen what I did to Egypt, and how I carried you as on eagle's wings and brought you to myself" (Ex. 19:4). Once again, as with Abraham and Adam, the Lord was encouraging them to have faith in Him by remembering His power and faithfulness.

Then, in light of this, the Lord God gave them their covenantal obligations. "Now if you obey me fully and keep my covenant, then out of all the nations you will be my treasured possession. Although the whole earth is mine, you will be for me a kingdom of priests and a holy nation" (Ex. 19:5). What Israel must do is the same as what Adam was supposed to do, and what Abraham did. They were to "obey God fully." They were to hear the Word of God and do it. Then the Lord attached a promise to the obligation by saying that if they obey the Lord God then they would be His "treasured possession - a holy nation." Just like with Adam and Abraham, the promise was connected to the obligation. *If* Adam would not eat from the forbidden tree, *then* he would continue to live in fellowship with his Lord. *If* Abraham would be willing to leave Haran, circumcise himself and his children, and ultimately, to sacrifice his one and only son, *then* he would receive the promise. Now the same covenantal promise was made: *if* Israel obeyed the Lord, *then* Israel would be the Lord's treasured possession. God is absolutely faithful because He will keep His covenantal promises. Covenantal history proves that this is not to be questioned. Now, in light of God's faithfulness, Israel must prove to be faithful in return, just as Abraham proved to be faithful even in the most difficult circumstances.

How would Israel be able to keep the covenant? How would Israel be able to "fully obey" as Abraham did? If we protest at this point by objecting, "Well, no one is able to fully obey, because nobody is perfect," then we have to deal with the Lord's own opinion of Abraham when He says, "Abraham obeyed me and kept my requirements, my commands, my decrees and my laws" (Gen. 26:5). Israel was being commanded to be like Abraham, nothing more and nothing less. Now, anyone remotely familiar with Abraham's life knows that Abraham was not perfect in the sense of being sinless. But Abraham, nevertheless kept the Lord's covenantal requirements.

So it follows that the Lord does not command perfection in the sense of sinless perfection, which becomes clear with the Lord's covenant with Israel. The Lord recognizes that men are sinful, and so He accounts for this within the covenant. The Lord dealt with the reality of sin with a "sin offering." When the community or an individual "becomes aware" of their sin, they are to bring a sin offering, a male goat without defect.[5] The guilty person was to confess their particular transgression, and then lay their hands on the head of the goat and simultaneously slaughter it. This represented the guilt being passed from the person to the goat and the punishment passes with the slaughtering of the goat. "In this way the priest will make atonement for the man's sin, and he will be forgiven" (Lev. 4:26). So it is possible to be someone who sins, and simultaneously "keeps the Lord God's requirements." In this way we see the graciousness of the Lord. This is why the Lord would proclaim about Himself to Moses, "The Lord, the Lord, the compassionate and gracious God, slow to anger, abounding in love and faithfulness, maintaining love to thousands, and forgiving wickedness, rebellion and sin" (Ex. 34:6, 7).

But we are now back to our original question. How would Israel be able to obey the Lord fully? They would be able to obey the Lord fully in the same way that Abraham was able to obey, Israel's keeping of the Lord's requirements would depend upon their faith in the Lord's Word to them. They would need to trust in God's faithfulness to keep His Word to be a merciful God. Would they believe God and then subsequently obey as Abraham did? Or would they fail to believe and consider God to be unreliable and miserly as Adam and Eve had? Just as Adam and Eve faced their testing, and just as Abraham received his great test, so the people of Israel would face their testings as well. Their faith or unbelief would be made known to the world by what they would do, by their obedience or lack thereof.

The promise for Israel was that they would be the Lord's treasured possession, but we need to look at this promise a little more closely. Isn't it true that Israel, Isaac's descendants, by virtue of God's covenant with Abraham, was *already* the Lord's treasured possession? Doesn't the fact the Lord saved them from Egypt in such a remarkable

---

5   This includes sins done with volition such as the breaking of a moral law. We see this in Leviticus chapters 5 and 6. There such sins as the failure to speak truthfully, thoughtlessly taking oaths, deceiving or cheating your neighbor or stealing are mentioned. The covenantal response was confession and sacrifice, then forgiveness is promised. Clearly these would not be sins done in ignorance since they all serve as a breach of one of the Ten Commandments, in that sense they are "intentional."

way demonstrate Israel's present status as God's people? Doesn't the very fact that the Lord is revealing His will specifically and explicitly to Israel mark them out as already being God's special people; His treasured possession, unlike all the other nations? The answer is yes.

In fact, Deuteronomy states, "But it was because the Lord *loved* you and kept the oath he swore to your forefathers that he brought you out with a mighty hand and redeemed you from the land of slavery, from the power of Pharaoh king of Egypt" (Deut. 7:8). The Lord already loves them! The fact that they are now His treasured possession is seen in His deliverance. Again, Deuteronomy, "For you *are* a people holy to the Lord your God. The Lord your God *has chosen you* out of all the peoples on the face of the earth to be his people, his treasured possession" (Deut. 7:6). Clearly, the Israelites, at the time of making the covenant at Sinai, were *already* God's "holy people," His "treasured possession." But this leads to a problem. If the Israelites were already God's treasured possession, why is this status given as a promise of something future in Exodus 19:5? How can it be that Israel *is* the Lord's treasured possession and at the same time they *will be* his treasured possession? The answer to this question is found in Exodus 20, in the Ten Commandments.

The Lord begins His covenantal statement by reminding His people of His past faithfulness, "I am the Lord your God, who brought you out of Egypt, out of the land of slavery." The Lord is *now* their God; He uniquely belongs to Israel. This is the great privilege of being a descendant of Abraham. Now the Lord lays out the covenantal obligations. "You shall have no other Gods, you shall not make idols, you shall not misuse the Lord's name." These are the first three commandments. The answer as to how Israel can already be the Lord's treasured possession, and still look forward to being so, is found embedded in the third commandment.

Within the third commandment the Lord inserts promised blessings for obedience and curses for disobedience. For those who sin and disregard these obligations the Lord promises punishment "to the third and fourth generation of those who hate me" (Ex. 20:5). But, He also promises "love to a thousand generations of those who love me and keep my commandments." Notice, he promises love! But doesn't He *already* love them? Yes, as we have seen, the Lord has loved Israel by choosing and delivering them. The point is that the covenant must be upheld or maintained. The Israelites must persevere in God's love *by*

28

continuing to love Him and keep His commands. The Israelites are now God's treasured possession, but they must persevere in obeying God fully in order to *remain* His treasured possession. The necessity to persevere in covenant loyalty allows the Lord to speak of both present and future experience of God's love. It is not as if the Israelites had to obtain something they didn't have, but like Adam and Abraham, they must persevere to remain in the existing relationship with the Lord. Once again, Deuteronomy states, "Know therefore that the Lord your God is God; he is the faithful God, *keeping* his covenant of love to a thousand generations of those who love him and keep his commands" (Deut. 7:9).

The covenant must be maintained, it must be kept in an ongoing way. We can illustrate this once again through marriage. When a woman commits herself to a man, she is vowing her love for him for life. The vow speaks of the future, of a commitment to maintain fidelity and covenant loyalty "till death do us part." This vow also incorporates times of hardship as a future possibility, "I love you now, but I will love you in the future even if I am tested by really hard things like sickness, disease and poverty." The importance of a vow is the future aspect. It is one thing to express a present love for someone, but it is the future that requires assurances; and a husband is a faithful husband by his record of covenant loyalty that is lasting. You can't be faithful for thirty years, then have an affair, and still be known as a faithful husband. Covenants by design require steadfastness. Covenants contain vows of allegiance. They speak of on-going relational fidelity. They only speak of the past as a way to provide assurances for the future.

The Lord reminds Israel about Egypt only to re-assure them that the land He promised Abraham is as good as theirs. But the covenant with the Lord is a gracious one, full of mercy. This would be similar to a situation when a woman marries a man knowing that he struggles with certain temptations. In light of this, the woman may have the man take an additional vow, "If you ever go astray, if you ever fall out of covenant loyalty, you must vow to come to me, weeping, repentant and hurting, for despising my love. And if you do, if your love for me is evident in your repentance, then I vow in return to keep you. You will remain mine and I will remain yours – not necessarily without repercussions and trials, but the covenant stands." Likewise, the covenant made with Israel at Sinai was a gracious and merciful covenant as expressed to Moses, "forgiving wickedness, rebellion and sin" (Ex. 34:7). When there is repentance there is mercy and even those who have been unfaithful can now be spoken of as faithful.

7.

The Lord God, Israel and the Great Divorce

The marriage covenant is an appropriate analogy to describe our covenant with God as it is this analogy that the Lord himself uses time and again in Scripture to describe His relationship with His people. Despite the Lord's covenant faithfulness, demonstrated over and over again, Israel by and large, would prove to be an unfaithful bride to her Lord. This is not to say that there were not loyal individuals and families within Israel; there were always some. But for the most part Israel could be described as unfaithful in fulfilling the covenant vows. As with Abraham, she would enter times of testing, but unlike Abraham, she would be quick to forget God's faithfulness of the past and fail to trust the Lord for her future. This was the tragic pattern of Israel's existence, destined to be repeated again and again.

This pattern of unfaithfulness was evident from the very beginning, right after she had been delivered from bondage in Egypt. During Israel's escape from captivity, as they stood on the shore of the Red Sea, the Lord tested their faith with a furious and rampaging Egyptian army, flying toward them across the desert. In that moment of duress and trial, the memory of the experience of the great power of their covenant Lord slipped their minds. They forgot about their God. In the terror that emanated from their unbelieving hearts, they cried out to Moses in angry sarcasm,

> Was it because there were no graves in Egypt that you brought us to the desert to die? What have you done to us by bringing us out of Egypt? Didn't we say to you in Egypt, "Leave us alone; let us serve the Egyptians"? It would have been far better for us to serve the Egyptians than to die in the desert (Ex. 14:11, 12).

31

Note the treachery within this statement. She had been delivered from murderous slavery in order to serve God, but now, in a moment of suffering and duress she was accusing her spouse of wanting her death. It was as if they were saying, "It would have been better for me never to have married!" Yet the Lord, in his grace, would overlook this treachery and use this moment as yet another powerful example of His abiding faithfulness. Israel would not need graves, but the Egyptian armed forces would need lots of them because of a dramatic and a memorable turn of events at the Red Sea.

Israel would celebrate her Lord's great faithfulness with exhilarated dancing and singing, because of this narrow escape from death. However, just as the plagues of God's deliverance were so easily forgotten in times of stress, thirst, terrible thirst in a bone-dry desert would drive the past faithfulness of her covenant Lord from her mind. For three days she traveled in the dry desert heat, without water. Suffering from thirst is tormenting, but their trial would only increase when they stumbled upon water at Marah, only to discover that it was not good to drink. Once again, unbelief would spill out in the form of complaint and angry grumbling. To complain is to question the goodness and ability of the Lord. Just as Adam and Eve doubted the Lord's goodness toward them, Israel followed suit. In response to this treachery of His people, once more the Lord demonstrated His covenant faithfulness by making the water clean and able to quench their thirst. Would Israel learn the lesson of God's faithfulness? Would she rest in the strength and love of her husband no matter what would come their way?

No, the treachery would continue. Like a long suffering and faithful husband, the Lord would continue to provide and protect His wife Israel, who would continue to complain and rebel. The Lord would carry her through the desert, providing water and bread in miraculous and powerful ways. In faithfulness the covenant Lord would lead her right to the threshold of the land He had promised Abraham and his descendants so many years ago. But once again, they would be frightened by what they experienced.

The people in the land that the Lord had promised them seemed too strong for them. Rather than believing the Lord's Word to give them the land, they believed instead that they would surely die in attempting what God had told them to do. Once again, the panic of unbelief overtook them. This time it would be so strong that the "whole assembly" planned to kill Moses and others, who by faith in God's promise, wanted to obey their Lord and invade the land. Inspired by this rank unbelief in God's gracious power to defeat their enemies, they now planned to murder Moses, and the others faithful to the Lord, as a way to save their own lives. In response to this infidelity of His people, Israel, the Lord said,

> How long will these people treat me with contempt? How long will these people refuse to believe in me, in spite of all the miraculous signs I have performed among them? I will strike them down with a plague and destroy them, but I will make you into a nation greater and stronger than they (Ex. 14:11, 12).

Israel, God's wife, had broken her vows of the marriage covenant since the beginning,while the Lord had been faithful to His vows. However, the Lord relented before the pleading of Moses and thus, He would maintain His painful allegiance to His unfaithful wife for almost another thousand years.

After that one thousand year period had passed, the Lord's patience would run out. His wife Israel had by this time strayed into numerous affairs with many other gods, something that was even rare among pagan nations. Usually, those nations were stubbornly loyal to their false gods, but Israel, in rebellion against the one true God, was more than willing to try any new god that seemed to be promising happiness and security (Jer. 2:10-12).

During the idolatrous reign of Manasseh in 698 B.C., the Lord determined that the breach was irreparable; Israel, as a nation, was now beyond forgiveness under the covenant made at Sinai. Even after Josiah's attempt to restore covenant faithfulness, 2 Kings 23:26 reports,

> Nevertheless, the Lord did not turn away from the heat of his fierce anger, which burned against Judah because of all that Manasseh had done to provoke him to anger. So the Lord said, "I will remove Judah also from my presence as I removed Israel, and I will reject Jerusalem, the city I chose, and this temple, about which I said, 'There shall my Name be.'"

Just as Adam and Eve had been cast out of God's presence in the garden, so Israel would be cast out of the Lord's presence. The prophet

Jeremiah would prophecy, "I gave faithless Israel her certificate of divorce and sent her away because of all her adulteries" (Jer. 3:8). Ezekiel would likewise prophecy using sexual metaphors to rebuke Israel, "Therefore this is what the Sovereign Lord says: Since you have forgotten me and thrust me behind your back, you must bear the guilt of your lewdness and prostitution" (Ez. 23:35). And Hosea revealed the Lord's hot and jealous anger,

> Rebuke your mother, rebuke her, for she is not my wife, and I am not her husband. Let her remove the adulterous look from her face and the unfaithfulness from between her breasts... I will not show my love to her children, because they are children of adultery. Their mother has been unfaithful and has conceived them in disgrace. She said, "I will go after my lovers, who will give me my food and my water, my wool and my linen, my oil and my drink" (Hos. 2:5).

Israel's pattern of behavior has been to trust in other gods, many other gods, for her protection and provision. She had lived a life of covenant breaking, and now the Lord Himself broke covenant with her, divorcing His chosen wife. This covenantal relationship was over and a great change had occurred. The writer of 2 Kings described the Lord as casting Israel out of His presence, while Ezekiel, who was with the exiles in Babylon, described this tragic event in another way. He, saw in a vision of the temple "the glory of the Lord depart from over the threshold of the temple" (Ez. 10:18). The Lord was casting the Israelites out of his presence by leaving them. No longer could the Lord bear to have His name slandered by His unfaithful wife. No longer could he tolerate her flagrant affairs and her lewd promiscuity. He was leaving and she would be left alone. She would face bitter and shameful destruction at the hands of those who never really loved her. She would go the way of her desires and she would reap the misery of her lust for others.

However, Israel was not left without hope, because the Lord promised He would return one day. And, after about 600 years, He would return. The Lord had made promises to Abraham and his descendants and despite the unfaithfulness of His wife, Israel, the Lord remained true to His Word. The promise to Abraham would be fulfilled and he would have a people, even a great nation. That great nation would have their land and all the peoples on earth would indeed be blessed through Abraham's seed. The Lord would return, and when He returns, He would be offering forgiveness for His repentant wife. The Old Covenant was broken, but He would start all over again with a New Covenant and a spotless Bride.

8.

Jesus Christ and the Return of the Covenant Lord

It is not insignificant that the first words spoken 600 years later, with the Lord's return to His people, would be "Repent, and believe the good news, the kingdom of God is at hand!" The first words spoken to Israel were very similar to those last words spoken by the prophets in the Old Covenant. John the Baptist and Jesus continued where Hosea, Joel, Amos, and others had left off hundreds of years earlier. The promises made about 2,000 years earlier in Genesis 12 were about to be kept. Hear the words of the prophet Micah, "You will be true to Jacob, and show mercy to Abraham, as you pledged on oath to our fathers in days long ago" (Mic. 7:20).

The Lord, Israel's husband, was returning to His pillaged and ravaged wife, and with His return He was expecting the appropriate response. He was expecting remorse, confession and lament from His unfaithful wife.

> "For your Maker is your husband - the Lord Almighty is his name - the Holy One of Israel is your redeemer; he is called the God of all the earth. The Lord will call you back as if you were a wife deserted and distressed in spirit - a wife who married young, only to be rejected," says your God. "For a brief moment I abandoned you, but with deep compassion I will bring you back" (Is. 54:5-7).

He has come willing to restore, forgive and reconcile. But forgiveness and reconciliation will not happen without repentance and confession. The wife, who has gone chasing after her lovers, must come to him humbled, renouncing her behavior. This is why the call of the kingdom is first and foremost a call to repentance, and why this is so pronounced

37

in John the Baptist's and Jesus' ministry (Mt. 3:1,2; 4:17). The Lord and Israel have a long history marred by one-sided covenantal infidelity, and that history must be recognized and accounted for.

However, it becomes increasingly apparent that the Lord was drawing more than just the nation of Israel to Himself. His plan includes more than ethnic Israel, because the Lord and the whole world have a history of the same one-sided infidelity going back to Adam. Throughout this history, the prophets had spoken about this return of the covenant Lord, not just for unfaithful Israel, but to show mercy to the unfaithful world.

Jesus Christ frequently revealed his mercy not just to the Israelite, but also to the pagan, as He was receiving not just the repentant and humble among the Jews, but also the repentant and humble among the Gentiles (Jn. 4:39-42; Mt. 8:11; 15:21-28). This was not on a whim. Jesus was not expressing a mercy that exceeded the mercy of the Lord in the Old Covenant, but this was a purposeful and intentional keeping of an oath which was reflected in the Old Covenant itself. This was part of the merciful promise that God had made to Abraham: "...and all peoples on earth will be blessed through you" (Gen. 12:3). Jesus was "the seed" of Abraham who was, at the very same time, the Lord of the covenant, who would be a blessing to all. Isaac, the son of Abraham, would produce in his line the one and only Son of God, as promised.

Jesus the covenant Lord, the Son of God, had returned to Israel in order to be a blessing to the whole world. The Presence of God had returned after departing from the temple in the vision of Ezekiel. The glory of the Lord had returned after having departed so many years ago and the apostle John would say, "We have seen his glory, the glory of the One and Only, who came from the Father full of grace and truth" (Jn. 1:14). The glory of the Lord would re-enter the Temple and find things not as they should be, so His wrath would break out in the form of whips and scathing rebukes (Mt. 21:12,13).

Jesus was the same covenant Lord who banned Adam and Eve from His presence in the garden, which is why Jesus could say with complete seriousness in John 8:58, "I tell you the truth, before Abraham was born, I am!" Jesus was the same covenant Lord who delighted exceedingly at Abraham's faithfulness in being willing to sacrifice his one and only son. It was with this same delight that Jesus would celebrate the faith of a Roman soldier who trusted Jesus' power and provision two thousand years later, "I tell you the truth, I have not found anyone in Israel with such great faith" (Mt. 8:10)! Jesus, the covenant Lord had now returned to His people, not as a fire-pot floating between the halves of sacrificed animals, nor as a pillar of fire by night and cloud by day, but as living, breathing, sweating, hungering and thirsting human being. "The Word became flesh and made his dwelling among us" (Jn. 1:14).

Jesus as the covenant Lord returned in order to reconcile Himself to an estranged world, to forgive and to set aside the sins of the past (Jn. 3:17). The whole world had gone astray since Adam, with Israel standing as the intensified and global witness to human sin. She had all the privileges and advantages, yet those remarkable and blessed advantages only served to magnify the power of human sin causing them to despise God and His provision (Rom. 3:1-4). God had removed any possible excuse for rebellion through the example of Israel (Rom. 3:19, 20). Adam stands as mankind's representative disobedient individual, while Israel stands as the representative disobedient nation. To gloat over Israel's destruction is to gloat over what the whole world deserves.

But now Jesus had come to set things right, to bring peace between God and mankind. How this could be accomplished was a mystery of great proportions to the Israel of Jesus' time (Mk. 4:11; Rom. 16:25). The Law and its sacrifice of animals could not take away the volitional, or willful guilt of human beings. In the Old Covenant, the Lord had promised forgiveness by these sacrifices and this was wonderfully true. Yet, it was ever-embedded in the consciousness of the Israelites that these animal deaths and sacrifices were not sufficient, that ultimately they could not justify a sinful man or woman. They knew the disparity between the guilt of human sins against a holy God, and the blood of animals as a rectifying remedy (Rom. 3:20; Heb. 10:1-3). When all the sacrifices had been performed, all the blood had been sprinkled, and all the fires had consumed their sacrificial victims, guilt remained in the soul of man It remained as a nagging cloud for even the most faithful Jew. In fact, the more faithful the Jew, the more he hungered for the ultimate consolation to be found only in the ultimate solution (Lk. 2:21-38). Jesus confirmed this hunger, "Blessed are those who hunger and thirst for righteousness, for they will be filled" (Mt. 5:6).

Yet the faithful Jew knew the Lord to be merciful and he, or she, would trust in the pronouncement given through temple observances even though they did not know *how* those pronouncements could be made. This was God's remedy as they had been taught. But they also knew well the promises of the prophets, that one day the Lord would deal finally and totally with the problem of sin and its residual guilt (Is. 40:1,2; Jer. 31:33,34). This is why some were waiting expectantly for the day of "consolation" when sins would finally be dealt with in such a way that only peace of mind remains.

Jesus' call for repentance and the announcement that the kingdom of God was at hand was continually confirmed by His performance of great miracles that would bring to mind the prophets Elijah and Elisha of long ago. He was healing and performing great signs among the unlikely as the prophets did in their day. He was making authoritative pronouncements that would sound very similar to Old Covenant Scriptures, yet would at times say more, causing Old Covenant teachers to blush and fume. Jesus did not make it His business to merely recite Old Covenant texts or to live strictly within their limits, but He made His own statements that were entirely new, yet bore a noticeable fragrance of the old.

His own claim was that He lived in absolute allegiance, not necessarily to the Law of Moses, but to His Father in heaven (Jn. 4:34; 17:8). He would say that He was "Lord of the Sabbath" (Mt. 12:8). He would claim freedom from the temple tax on the basis of His Son-ship to the Father (Mt. 17:24). He would stand as His own witness, claiming a unique right to do so (Jn. 8:17,18). He seemed to be a walking and talking authoritative Word unto Himself (Mt. 7:28, 29).

As with the Lord's call to Abram generations before, the Lord would issue His call once again, now through Jesus Christ. Jesus would stop, fix His gaze on certain individuals and call them to "follow me." They, in turn, immediately dropped what they were doing, and went with Him. Now, it is true that some preparation had been made for these calls to discipleship. We have no need to make them more than what they were, because what they were is enough. These were not moments of radical existential choice made in a vacuum of knowledge.[6]

---

6 Bonhoeffer seems concerned to negate any possibility of prior exposure to Jesus in order to promote an understanding of faith that derives from existentialist philosophy. For Bonhoeffer, to have faith is to act against reason by definition. The disciples to have true faith must be confronted by an existential moment of genuine choice that has had no outside influence, they can have no reasons outside of a "raw" existential moment with God. But as we see with Abraham in Genesis

Peter, Andrew, James and John very likely had heard Jesus and seen His power before His call to them (Jn. 1:35-42). The whole area was alive with talk about Jesus and the significance of what He was saying and doing. So when Jesus turned to them individually and beckoned them to follow, it was their faith in whom Jesus was that enabled them to obey His call without question. They were able to follow because they had heard and seen, and because they had heard and seen, they believed, and because they believed, like Abraham before, they obeyed His command to follow Him, leaving family and livelihood behind and putting their lives squarely in His hands.

As Abraham's faith was tested, so would the disciple's faith be tested. They would be without food in desert places, they would be caught in violent storms, and they would be vilified and rejected as apostates and false teachers. However, the greatest test of all would be the shameful and humiliating crucifixion of their Lord, for whom they had left everything. Like the Israelites who cried out in fear at the edge of the Red Sea, they would not fare well; the "sheep would be scattered" at the capture and death of their shepherd.

But for them, the great test of Jesus' death was not to be the end of the story, but rather the beginning, just as it was for the Israelites. It was in the midst of Israelite infidelity at the Red Sea that God's righteous deliverance shone forth with special brightness. He vindicated His name and His people in one decisive moment, and stood justified as true to His promise to deliver, and His righteousness was revealed. It was an act that was to end all doubt and to seal, in the minds of the Israelites, God's invincible faithfulness to His Word.

Likewise, it was in the midst of the frightened and disillusioned disciples, that God's righteous deliverance and perfect faithfulness would shine; Christ, raised from the dead, would stand utterly victorious over sin and death. Men had thrown all they could at Him, had tormented and killed the Lord God in the most horrific way. But Jesus would stand in the midst of His disciples, justified as true to His promise to be raised victorious. He was vindicated as God's One and Only (1 Tim. 3:16). All that He had said was now to be understood as true. His appearance among them was to remove all doubt, silence all

---

22 and as explained by Hebrews 11, this is an unbiblical philosophical assumption. To act by faith is to do the most reasonable thing in light of the reality of God's promises and prior exposure to God's faithfulness. To have faith in the present is to act according to true reason.

protest, and usher in unshakable faith (Jn. 20:26, 27;1; Jn. 1:1-4). The "new exodus" was now underway. The lamb had been slain, the enemy had been defeated, and the way to life was now revealed (Is. 43:16-21; 51:9-11; Jn. 14:6,7).

But we must back up, and take a closer look at what Jesus said prior to His death by way of covenantal Words to His followers. We must return to Jesus' final Passover meal in which He ushered in the New Covenant. It was in the context of the Old Covenant Passover that the New Covenant Passover commences. Just as the Old Covenant people lived in a relationship characterized by privileges and obligations, so do the Lord's New Covenant people.

9.

Jesus Christ and His New Covenant

History is marked by crucial moments of the Lord God entering into covenantal relationship with man. That is, He enters into a relationship which consists of the establishment of privileges and obligations. Adam and Eve had the wonderful privilege of life with the Lord's unmitigated presence and the happiness of a creation fashioned just for them. They also had responsibilities, or obligations, to the Giver of life; they were responsible to watch over and care for God's creation and not to eat from a particular tree. The continued enjoyment of these privileges was conditional upon their continued keeping of their responsibilities or, obligations. *If* they remained faithful to the Lord, *then* they would remain in God's abundant blessing.

We saw the same conditional relationship with Abraham. He had the wonderful privilege of a great future of blessing. A great nation would come from his descendants and they had the promise of a vast and fruitful land to enjoy. As with Adam, these privileges were conditioned upon keeping obligations. Abraham had to obey the Lord God when He spoke. The promises would be his *if* he obeyed God and left his home, *if* he obeyed the Lord in circumcising his descendants, and last but not least, *if* he would be willing to sacrifice his one and only son. *If* Abraham was willing to trust the Lord and walk in faithfulness, *then* the promises would be his.

This was the same covenantal arrangement that the Lord made with Abraham's descendants at Sinai. Through Moses, the Lord promised to remain as their Lord; the Lord who would carry Israel as on eagle's wings. He would be their very own shield and their very great reward. The people of Israel would likewise continue to be the Lord's "treasured possession." This was the covenantal privilege. They would remain a blessed people *if* they would in turn be faithful to the

Lord and keep His commands and His ways.

These were the covenantal obligations. This is how a relationship with the Lord functioned under the Old Covenant. Does the New Covenant function in the same way? Do we continue to understand our relationship to the Lord to be a conditional one in which the enjoyment of the privileges are dependent upon the keeping of obligations? To answer this crucial question we must join Jesus with His disciples in the upper room only a few hours before He would be sacrificed by Roman crucifixion.

The final hours before Jesus' death were thick with the intensity of His final preparations for His departure. First, Jesus taught self-surrendering love as His will for the disciples in the shocking demonstration of the washing of their feet before the Passover meal, when Jesus took on the role of a slave (Jn. 13:1-17). Second, He celebrated the Passover, but now investing the Passover feast with new meaning, which was something no mere man could conceivably do. Two of the elements used in the Jewish Passover celebration, unleavened bread and wine, were employed by Jesus to remind the disciples of His broken body rather than the exodus events of the Old Covenant. Third, Jesus engaged them with teaching, consisting of commands and promises.

Nowhere, except in the Sermon on the Mount, is there recorded in the Gospels such a sustained discourse from Jesus as there is from John 14 through John 16. This is most appropriate, because Jesus had just done something that would have caught the ear of any first century Jew and have them sitting up straight. He had just ratified a New Covenant during the eating of the Passover meal. As we have seen, with covenant making comes the issuing of covenant privileges and obligations. If Jesus had just announced a New Covenant without the announcement of privileges and obligations, then the disciples would have been left in a fog. So just as the Lord had set promises and commandments, privileges and obligations before Adam, Abraham and Moses, so now Jesus, the Lord in human flesh, does the same.

Just as Moses reminded the Israelites of God's unfailing love generations earlier, in the few hours before his death, the Lord Jesus reminded His disciples of His constant love shown to them over the past three years. They have had the tremendous privilege of being called to Him, and to share in His power, protection and provision. The Lord did this for the twelve tribes of Israel in summary fashion at Sinai when He said, "You yourselves have seen what I did to Egypt, and how I carried you on eagles' wings and brought you to myself" (Ex. 19:4). This statement summarizes all that the Lord had done to protect and provide for Israel.

In the upper room, Jesus reminded the twelve disciples, in the same way, when He said, "As the Father has loved me, so have I loved you" (Jn. 15:9). Jesus' love for them had been experienced in tangible acts of calling, protection, provision and the revelation of God's will. "I have revealed you to those whom you gave me out of the world... For I gave them the words you gave me and they accepted them" (Jn. 17:6,8). Also, Jesus prayed to the Father, "While I was with them I protected them and kept them safe by that name you gave me" (Jn. 17:12). So just as in the Old Covenant, the New Covenant begins by recalling the Lord's history of faithfulness and love. Jesus had demonstrated His love for His people and they were now His "treasured possession."

Next, Jesus instructs them on how they are to remain His treasured possession, or as He put it, how they are to remain in His love. "If you obey my commands, you will remain in my love, just as I have obeyed my Father's commands and remain in His love" (Jn. 15:10). Here we find the covenantal obligations. Jesus' words to His disciples are His commands to them, that are to be kept and by which they are to remain in the privilege of His love. We must note that *remaining* by virtue of their call to follow is not what is taught by Jesus. Jesus presents the need to remain as a *command*, which is something they are to do *subsequent to their call to follow Him*. Jesus said, "Remain in me, and I will remain in you" (Jn. 15:4). They were to remain in Jesus by obeying His commands. As they obey Jesus, His love will continue to be theirs. The logic of Jesus' reasoning is covenantal in nature, and is exactly the same as what we have seen before in the Lord's covenant with Adam, Abraham and Moses. Note the obvious parallels in the following passages:

> I will make you descendants as numerous as the stars in the sky and will give them all these lands, and through your offspring all nations on earth will be blessed, *because* Abraham obeyed me and kept my requirements, my commands, my decrees and my laws (Gen. 26:4).

I, the Lord your God, am a jealous God, punishing the children for the sin of the fathers to the third and fourth generation of those who hate me, but showing love to a thousand generations of those who love me and keep my commandments (Ex 20:5).

As the Father has loved me, so have I loved you. Now remain in my love. If you obey my commands you will remain in my love, just as I have obeyed my Father's commands and remain in His love. I have told you this so that my joy may be in you and that your joy may be complete. My command is this: Love each other as I have loved you (Jn 15:9-14).

In all three passages we are able to clearly discern that the privilege of being loved and blessed by the Lord is dependent upon meeting the obligations of the covenant. It was *because* Abraham obeyed the Lord that he was able to receive the promise (Gen. 26:4). It was *by* loving God and keeping His commandments that Israel would experience God's love and not His hatred (Ex. 20:5). Jesus taught His disciples in the same way.

It was *by* obeying Jesus that the disciples would not experience His hatred, or as He graphically put it, be "cut off" and "thrown into the fire and burned," but rather, they would "experience His love, and be filled with joy" forever (Jn. 15:2, 6, 11). As the writer of Hebrews proclaims, "Jesus Christ is the same yesterday and today and forever" (Heb. 13:8). The covenant Lord does not change like shifting shadows. God relates the same way with His people in every age. He demonstrates Himself as an infinitely faithful Lord, committing Himself in total to His people, even dying for them as necessity dictates. "Greater love has no one than this, that he lay down His life for His friends" (Jn. 15:13).

However, the covenant *requires* faithfulness in return. This was true of the Old Covenant and is equally true of the New Covenant. On this Jesus is abundantly clear. "If anyone would come after me, he must deny himself and take up his cross and follow me. For whoever wants to save his life will lose it, but whoever loses his life for me will find it" (Mt. 16:24, 25). The writer of Hebrews states, "You *need to persevere* so that when you have done the will of God, you will receive what he has promised" (Heb. 10:36). In these passages we hear very clear echoes of the total allegiance required in the Old Covenant. The reason is equally clear; God's covenantal requirements are the same—total allegiance from both parties is required. He guarantees faithfulness to us, even to the point of His own death. We must be faithful in return, even to the point of experiencing our own death, if required, in allegiance to Him.

Once again, total allegiance does not imply sinless perfection. The Lord covenants with His people knowing that we are sinful by nature. Both the Old and New Covenants take our sinful condition into account. God's covenant is fundamentally a gracious one and based on mercy. God was merciful in calling Abram, Israel and His disciples to be His people. Under the Old Covenant, as we have seen, sin offerings were made, along with confession of sins committed, and the people would then receive God's gracious pardon. This was part and parcel of what it meant to have total allegiance to the Lord, by confessing sin and subsequently turning away from that sin to the ways of the Lord. This expression of total allegiance was to be repeated according to the dictates of the covenant and according to individual necessity.

According to Hebrews 7:26-28, the New Covenant requires the same pattern of confession, except there is now no longer any need to present a sin offering. Jesus, as the New Covenant Passover makes clear, is the once-for-all spotless lamb, the final and all-sufficient sin offering. Heb. 6:13-20 explains how the Lord Himself would take on the guilt and punishment for our sins as the fulfillment of His covenantal vow to Abraham described in Genesis 15; the Lord Jesus Christ would bear the penalty of our unfaithfulness. From Heb. 9:13, 14, we now know *how* the Lord is able to forgive sins, and our consciences can be cleansed and set at rest, as they could not be under the Old Covenant.

It is wonderfully true that since Jesus presented Himself as the final all-sufficient sacrifice we no longer have need to present offerings. Nevertheless, it remains a covenantal mandate to confess and turn from sin as an expression of our total allegiance to the Lord within the covenant. That aspect has not changed. This is why Jesus instructs his disciples to pray asking for their sins to be forgiven as part of a covenantal prayer. "Forgive us our debts, as we have also forgiven our debtors" (Mt. 6:12). This is why John instructs the church, God's New Covenant people, "If we confess our sins, he is faithful and just and will forgive us our sins and purify us from all unrighteousness" (1 Jn. 1:9). That is why the writer of Hebrews exhorts the church to "draw near to God with a sincere heart in full assurance of faith, having our hearts sprinkled to cleanse us from a guilty conscience and having our bodied washed with pure water" (Heb. 10:22).

It is a mistake to think that we don't need a sacrifice or a High Priest anymore; we still need both. In the New Covenant, this means we need Jesus, who now functions as both the High Priest and as a cleansing sacrifice for His people. And it is not to say that we don't *need* on-going confession of sin in order to remain in Christ's love. That aspect of the covenant remains a fundamental expression of covenant loyalty to our Lord as Jesus, as John and the writer of Hebrews makes abundantly clear.

The conditional nature of the New Covenant is explicit, "*If* we confess our sins, [*then*] He is faithful and just and will forgive us our sins..." (1 Jn. 1:9). *If* we are faithful to confess, to be honest and not deceitful toward the Lord, *then* He in turn will be faithful to do what He has promised, He will forgive us. We will keep the commands of Jesus in the same way that Abraham kept the commands of the Lord, by faith in all that the Lord has promised. Abraham obeyed by faith in the promises of the Lord and we are to do the same. Abraham had to obey in order to receive the promise, and so must we.

The only way we will obey Jesus even to the point of dying, if necessary, is by having confidence in the truthfulness of Jesus when He promises us,

> Do not let your hearts be troubled. Trust in God, trust also in me. In my Father's house there are many rooms; if it were not so I would have told you. I am going there now to prepare a place for you, I will come back and take you to be with me that you may also be where I am (Jn. 14:1-3).

Jesus intends us to rest by faith in those words, so that we would obey all Jesus said, no matter what opposition comes our way. The worst thing anyone can do to someone who is faithful to Jesus is to send them to the very place they most want to be - with Jesus in His kingdom, as the writer of Psalm 27 proclaims, "One thing I ask of the Lord, that is what I seek: that I may dwell in the house of the Lord all the days of my life, and gaze upon the beauty of the Lord and to seek him in his holy temple" (Ps. 27:4). Since this is true, then the Psalmist can also speak with confidence, "The Lord is the stronghold of my life - of whom shall I be afraid" (Ps. 27:1)? These are covenantal words of faith in the Lord's perfect faithfulness. These expressions of faith are able to be expressions that are reflective of both Old and New Covenant loyalty and desire, because both covenants require loyalty to the Lord, and uphold God Himself as the chief object of our desire.

10.

Paul, the Apostle of the New Covenant

The Apostle Paul considered himself to be a "minister of a New Covenant" (2 Co. 3:6), the same covenant that Jesus instituted through the Passover meal with his disciples in the upper room. Even though Paul had not been present at that meal, he was personally taught by Jesus, the Resurrected Lord, about the meal and its significance for God's people. Paul wrote, "For what I received from the Lord I passed on to you: The Lord Jesus, on the night he was betrayed, took bread, and when he has given thanks, he broke it and said..." (1 Co. 11:23, 24). In Acts 9, we learn that Paul, who was named Saul at the time, experienced the Lord, when on the road to Damascus to persecute those who belonged to the Way. Jesus knocked him off his horse and blinded him, after which Saul spent considerable time being taught, not by men, but by the post resurrection Lord (Gal. 1:17,18). This first-hand experience with Jesus qualified him to be an apostle of the New Covenant, along with the original eleven apostles and Matthias.

We have seen how the Lord has related to His people covenantally from the very beginning. We have also seen that the Lord communicates with His people in covenantal ways as an expression of that relationship. This covenantal relationship is reflected at Mount Sinai, in the Old Testament, where the Lord calls the people to remember His power and provision as tangible expressions of His faithfulness in the past. He did this in order that they trust in the Lord for their future, and by trusting Him, keep His commands and requirements during the present time.

We saw how Jesus, in the upper room, did the same thing. The previous three years of His ministry served as a reference point of Jesus' faithful ability to keep His promises for the future. In view of His mercies in the past, He commands His followers to obey Him, in the present, as they trust Him for the future. So what we see taking shape is a three-fold communication that captures the *past, present,* and the *future.*[7]

Looking back at God's past actions, enables us to have faith in God's word for the future, so that we are free to obey in the present. "I run in the paths of your commands, for you have set my heart free" (Ps. 119:32). The focus of the covenant is on the day to day faithfulness, which is crucial in order to remain in God's love. To put it another way, looking back, to see God's faithfulness in the past, serves to uphold and enable faith in God's word of promise for the future. Faith in God's word of promise for the future serves to uphold today's obedience. Or, to put it more succinctly, faith serves to establish obedience.

Let me illustrate this covenant dynamic. When my daughter was little she would stand on the stairs and jump into my arms. After jumping into my arms, she would climb up a little higher and jump again. Finally, she would reach a point where she was very nervous about jumping. She would hold her arms out, but she wouldn't quite dare to take that leap. In order to encourage her to jump, I would remind her that in the past I caught her every time that she had jumped. Then I would promise her, that if she jumped from this height that I would catch her this time as well. I was motivating her to jump by having her recall the past, and on the basis of the past, I was encouraging her to trust me for her future safety. The point was to produce the action of jumping in the present.

Likewise, the covenantal structure serves the purpose of establishing the daily walk of faithfulness. This daily walk is all-important in our relationship with God. Jesus says, "If anyone would come after me, he must deny himself and take up his cross *daily* and follow me" (Lk. 9:23). The writer of Hebrews, in quoting the Psalms, teaches this day to day covenantal focus of both covenants, "*Today,* if you hear his voice, do not harden your hearts" (Heb. 4:7b; Ps. 95:7,8).

The apostle Paul understood his ministry to be one which establishes people in this daily faithfulness to Jesus. He understood faith to be crucial for enabling obedience to the commands of Jesus. This perspective is revealed in a succinct phrase used by Paul to open and close his letter to the church in Rome. Paul understood his mission from Christ to call the Gentiles to, as he puts it, an "obedience of faith" (Rom. 1:5; 16:26; 1 Th. 1:3). He saw it as his task to call the Gentiles

---

7 I am particularly indebted to Scott Hafemann for this observation, which can be found in *The God of Promise and the Life of Faith.* Crossway, 2001, 56-59.

into a covenant with the living God. "Through him and for his name sake, we received grace and apostleship to call people from among all the Gentiles to the *obedience of faith*" (Rom. 1:5). The fact that Paul uses this phrase in the opening paragraph of his letter and again in the final paragraph indicates the importance of this concept for Paul, and points to the main theme of his letter to the church.

When Paul wrote his letters to the churches, he was either addressing a particular problem in a church, or he was writing a more general teaching that was to be circulated to all the other churches. In these more general letters we see an implicit covenantal structure emerge. We see this structure in Paul's letters to Rome, Ephesus, Colosse, Philippi, and Thessalonica in particular.[8] There is a pattern to his writings that reflects our covenantal relationship with the Lord, just as the Old Covenant writings reflected this relationship.

In Paul's letters, the first portion describes God's past acts of faithfulness on behalf of the world and His people. A cursory reading of Ephesians 1-3 reveals this emphasis. In the first portion of his letter, Paul spends most of his energy describing what spiritual condition the people were in before Christ, and all that Christ has done for them. "As for you, *you were dead* in your transgressions and sins, in which *you used to live...* But because of his great love for us, God, who is rich in mercy, *made us alive with Christ....*" (Eph. 2:1, 4). The past is the focus. In fact, in Ephesians, Paul reaches back to the pre-creation past in describing the Lord's great love. "Praise be to the God and Father of our Lord Jesus Christ, *who has blessed us* in the heavenly realms with every spiritual blessing in Christ. For *he chose us in him* before the creation of the world to be holy and blameless in his sight" (Eph. 1:3, 4).

However, in chapter 4 we can discern a pronounced shift in focus. The focus now shifts to commanding the Ephesians' present

---

8 It is interesting to note that Paul was generally pleased with these churches, and he was not caught up in the pointed and polemic demands of churches in danger of going astray, as in Corinth and Galatia. James Dunn notes this in reference to Paul's letter to Rome, "...there is one letter of Paul's which is less caught in the flux and developing discourse of Paul with his churches than the others... in short, Romans is still far removed from a dogmatic or systematic treatise on theology, but it nevertheless is the most sustained and reflective statement of Paul's own theology by Paul himself" (*The Theology of Paul the Apostle,* Eerdmans, 2006, 25). This, I believe, can be said of other letters as well. It is with these "sustained and reflective statements of Paul's own theology" where the covenantal structure is most clearly visible.

obedience and faithfulness to the Lord.

> As a prisoner of the Lord, therefore, I urge you *to live a life worthy* of the calling you have received.... So I tell you this, and insist on it in the Lord, that *you must no longer live as the Gentiles do*, in the futility of their thinking....*Be imitators of God* therefore, as dearly loved children and *live a life of love,* just as Christ loved us... Be very careful *how you live*... Finally, *be strong in the Lord* and in his mighty power (Eph. 4:1, 17; 5:1, 15; 6:10).

From chapter 4 onward, the behavior of God's people in the present is front and center. The emphasis becomes what the Ephesians must do *now* in light of God's past mercies.[9]

Paul closes his letter with a patently covenantal statement, "Grace to all who love our Lord Jesus Christ with an undying love" (Eph. 6:24). Who is to receive the grace of Christ's love? Those who love Christ! What emerges is Paul thinking and writing covenantally. He celebrates God's past faithfulness in the first portion of his letter, then he exhorts the people of God to be faithful to their Lord with such words as "be worthy of the calling." How are we to be "worthy" of God's faithfulness? The same way the Israelites were to be deemed worthy under the Old Covenant, by being faithful to our Lord in loving God and neighbor. Then Paul closes the letter with a promise of grace for those who love Jesus in this way. This is identical to what was written in the Ten Commandments, "but showing love to a thousand generations of those who love me" (Ex. 20:6).

This very same pattern is seen in Paul's letter to the church in Rome. The first eleven chapters of Romans review the world's fall into sin, and the Lord's faithfulness in acting powerfully through Christ to save and redeem the resulting rebellious world. Paul highlights those men of the past, Abraham and David, who lived lives of faith, rejoicing

---

9   Typically, this shift in Paul's focus has been called a shift from theological or theoretical material in the first section of Paul's letters, to pastoral, practical or ethical material in the latter portions. This is not how we should think about Paul's writings. The first portions are every bit as pastoral, ethical and practical as the latter portions, and the latter portions are every bit as theological as the first. The covenant reveals why and how this is true, since the first portions report God's faithfulness to us, and the latter portions require our faithfulness to Him in response.

in God's righteousness. "Against all hope, *Abraham in hope believed and so became the father of many nations*" (Rom. 4:18). Paul highlights Adam as a man of unfaithfulness, and describes how sin entered the world through him. "Therefore, just as *sin entered the world* through the one man, and death through sin, and in this way *death came to all men....*" (Rom. 5:12).

Paul then records how Christ in His obedience redeemed the world through His death and resurrection, which was a powerful and redemptive event. "For if the many died by the trespass of the one man, how much more *did God's grace and the gift that came by the grace of the one man, Jesus Christ, overflow* to the many" (Rom. 5:15)! Just like in the letter to the Ephesians, in Romans 9, Paul reaches back in time to God's electing grace as being God's decision to save whom He will, "Just as it is written, 'Jacob I loved, but Esau I hated'" (Rom. 9:13). So we see that Romans 1-11 is, for the most part, a chronicle of the Lord's past righteousness and faithfulness, just like the first chapters of Deuteronomy. The following comparison of Moses' covenantal communication and Paul's in Romans, should clearly show the strong similarity.

In the first three chapters of Deuteronomy, Moses wrote a chronicle of God's past faithfulness and Israel's unfaithfulness. This is done intentionally as a covenantal way of inspiring faith in the Lord, as if to say, "Look at all that the Lord *has done* for us!" This is exactly what Paul is doing in Romans. He is writing a letter in which the first portion is to inspire the Christians in Rome to have faith in God. The Israelites under the Old Covenant were to look back at God's wonders since their exodus out of Egypt. "The Lord your God *has blessed you* in all the work of your hands. He *has watched over* your journey through this vast desert. These forty years the Lord your God *has been with you*, and *you have not lacked* anything" (Deut. 2:7). Paul has the people think back to Jesus. "He who *did not spare* his own Son, but *gave him up* for us all - how will he not also, along with him, graciously give us all things" (Rom. 8:32)? Notice how Paul directs the people to remember God's profound faithfulness in surrendering Christ to death on their behalf in order to inspire faith in God for the future. In other words, "if God has acted in this way in the past, how can we *not* trust Him for our future?"

After Moses spends the first three chapters of Deuteronomy in remembrance, the focus noticeably shifts in chapter 4. Moses shifts from describing God's faithfulness in the past, to commanding Israel's faithfulness to the Lord in the present. *"Hear now,* O Israel, the decrees and laws I am about to teach you. *Follow them* so that you may live and may go in and take possession of the land that the Lord, the God of your fathers, is giving you" (Deut. 4:1). This is precisely what Paul does in Romans chapter 12. The focus shifts from God's faithfulness in the past, to commanding the church's faithfulness in the present. "Therefore, *I urge you,* brothers, in view of God's mercy, to *offer your bodies* as living sacrifices, holy and pleasing to God - *this is your spiritual act of worship"* (Rom. 12:1). From chapter 12 onward, the focus is on the commands to be kept.

> Love must be sincere... share with God's people who are in need... Practice hospitality... Do not be conceited... Do not repay anyone evil for evil... Do not be overcome by evil, but overcome evil with good... Everyone must submit himself to the governing authorities... Give everyone what you owe him... pay taxes... Accept him whose faith is weak... let us stop passing judgment on each other... let us make every effort to do what leads to mutual edification... Accept one another as Christ has accepted you... I urge you, brothers, to watch out for those who cause divisions and put obstacles in your way... keep away from them (Rom. 12:9, 13, 16, 17, 21; 13:1,7; 14:1, 13,1 9; 15:7; 16:17).

As this comparison makes clear, the structure of the New Covenant is exactly the same structure as in the Old Covenant. In both covenants, the past provides the reference point from which we are able to trust the Lord's promises for the future. Faith in God's Word to us is the means by which we are to obey the Lord's commands. And, it is by obedience to the Lord that He fulfills His promises to us, just as He did with Abraham.

The Lord Jesus promises to love us as His people, *if* we love Him by obeying His commands. He promises to forgive us as we forgive others in obedience to His command to forgive. He promises to be merciful as we are merciful to others. And, Jesus promises us forgiveness, mercy and steadfast love. How are we to experience this forgiveness, mercy and steadfast love? *By* obeying His commands to be forgiving, loving and merciful. He will forgive us *because* we have forgiven others. He will be merciful to us *because* we have been merciful to others. And, He we love us *because* we have loved others. We will be loved, forgiven and be shown mercy on the basis of our faithfulness to Jesus. How will we be able to obey Jesus in forgiving others, in being merciful to others, in loving others?[10] We will be able to obey Jesus by trusting His promises to bless us with forgiveness, mercy and love! Our own lives are at stake in the way we deal with others.

The covenant motivates us to faithfulness as we understand that God's faithfulness to bless us is dependent upon our faithfulness to Jesus. As the apostle Paul wrote, "Grace to all who love our Lord Jesus Christ with an undying love" (Eph. 6:24). Who will experience the grace of Jesus' love, mercy and forgiveness? All who love Jesus by obeying his commands. Because Jesus Himself says, "Whoever has my commands and obeys them, he is the one who loves me. He who loves me will be loved by my Father, and I too will love him and show myself to him" (Jn. 14:21).

---

10 I assume that it is by the gracious work of the Spirit alone, that we both believe and obey God. This book is about how the covenant functions, but I grant joyfully and wholeheartedly that "God works in us to will and to do" (Php. 2:13).

11.

The Lord God's Covenant is To Be Obeyed by Faith

We have observed thus far that the Lord's gracious covenant with His people consists of both promises to be believed and commands to be obeyed. What we have also seen is that obedience is dependent upon faith, and faith's purpose is to enable obedience or faithfulness. The one is not to exist without the other. Faith is never to stand alone, because its very purpose is to make us obedient. To have faith standing alone is to deny the purpose for faith within the covenant. True obedience cannot exist without faith. As Dietrich Bonhoeffer has said, "Only those who obey can believe, and only those who believe can obey."[11]

We will never be able do the kinds of things the Lord commands us to do without believing the promises He has given us. It would simply be impossible. Let me give you an example from the Lord's command for us to "love our enemies." Jesus has explained, in Scripture, that the person who loves those who love them is nothing unique, the whole world behaves in this way and recognizes the obligation to love those who love us. We have popular sayings that reflect this, such as "one good turn deserves another" and "you scratch my back and I will scratch yours." In other words, "you do good to me and I will do good to you." These are popular sayings because it is what everyone recognizes as being fair and just.

But Jesus commands us, as His covenantal people, to do something that is unnatural, to "love your enemies and pray for those who persecute you." This is love of the most *uncommon* kind and proves that the Lord's covenant is not just "common sense," but goes

---

11 Bonhoeffer, *The Cost of Discipleship,* 76.

beyond mere human reasoning (Rom. 5:6-8). We see the unity of the Scriptures when His apostle Paul commands the same thing in Romans 12:14, "Bless those who persecute you; bless and do not curse."

But how are we to "bless them"? Jesus has already given us one way to love them: He instructs us to pray for them. Paul gives us other ways, quoting Proverb 25;21, 22. He says to "feed him if he is hungry" and to "give him something to drink if he is thirsty." In other words, we are to act toward enemies *as if* they are our friends. They are to experience the love of friendship even though no true friendship exists. This is not so simple! When someone is making our lives difficult and actively pursuing our ruin, everything within us cries out to retaliate. After all, they would only be getting what they deserve, right? There is nothing more difficult for a Christian to do than what Jesus and Paul mandate. We are to give people what they do not deserve. How are we to do it?[12] How are we to love those who curse us by their words and actions? We are to do it by faith.

Here again we see the covenant at work. Jesus has given us a life-giving promise that we are to hold on to with all our might. Right after he calls us to uncommon love for enemies, he motivates us by saying, "that you may be sons of your Father in heaven" (Mt. 5:45). The Father promises that we *will be* His sons. We will be received and welcomed as His children. But in order to receive this promise, we must obey the command to be like our Father. For the Father loves those who hate him everyday, as He causes the sun to shine, and the rain to fall on the earth, causing the earth to bring forth its abundance for the good of all people. In the same way, we must love those who hate us. So we take Jesus at His Word and because we want to be sons of the Father, we obey His command. By faith in the promise for the future we are to obey the Father in the present. Our very sonship is at stake, and this is the most powerful motivation to perform what has been commanded.

Paul motivates us to love our enemies as well. He does so by promising God's future vengeance upon the evil and spiteful people of the world. "'It is mine to avenge; I will repay,' says the Lord" (Rom. 12:19). This is God's covenantal promise. Justice will fall and no one who is found guilty of wrong-doing will escape. Therefore, "Do not take revenge, my friends, but leave room for God's wrath" (Rom. 12:19). We bless and not curse because it is God's job to do the cursing,

---

12 See footnote 9.

and He will do it perfectly. We are to trust the Word of the Lord for justice, and by trusting God's promise, we are to do good to *all* people. In fact, Paul makes clear through Proverbs 25:21, 22, that our doing good to our enemies will turn out to be greater warrant for God's punishment of them. The ignored love that we show to our enemies will serve to increase their judgment in the day of God's promised wrath. This is the reasoning behind Paul's statement, "In doing this, you will heap burning coals on his head" (Rom. 12:20). For Paul and Jesus, we are to obey these uncommon commands by faith in our Lord's Word of promise for the future. Without faith, this kind of obedience will be impossible, and without obedience, we become the evil and vindictive ones who are subject to what our enemies deserve. I, with my enemies, become an enemy of God. So Paul commands the church in Rome, "Do not be overcome by evil, but overcome evil with good" (Rom. 12:21).

So as we can see, the covenant holds faith and obedience together as an organic unity. This is reflected by passages in both the New Testament and the Old Testament, and it is equally true of both covenants. Note the unity of faith and obedience reflected in the following passages:

"Then they would put their *trust* in God and would not forget his deeds, but would *keep his commands*" (Ps. 78:7).

"Good will come to him who is *generous* and *lends freely*, who *conducts his affairs with justice*... He will have no fear of bad news; his heart is steadfast, *trusting* in the Lord" (Ps. 112:5,7).

"Who among you fears the Lord and *obeys* the word of his servant? Let him who walks in the dark, who has no light, *trust* in the name of the Lord and rely on his God" (Is. 50:10).

"Whoever *believes* in the Son has eternal life, but whoever *disobeys* the Son will not see life, for God's wrath remains on him" (Jn. 3:36).

"Who were they who heard and rebelled? Were they not all those Moses led out of Egypt? And with whom was he angry for forty years? Was it not with those who sinned, whose bodies fell in the desert? And to whom did God swear that they would not enter his rest if not those who *disobeyed*? So we see that they were not able to enter because of their *unbelief"* (Heb. 3:16 -19).

These passages reflect the reality of the Lord's covenant with His people. It is true, we can certainly think about "faith" in isolation from obedience. We can take the experience of faith and put it under a microscope and analyze it as it stands alone. We can take a theoretical look at "faith alone," and we can do the same with obedience, or with works. But we cannot understand faith alone, or works alone, and understand either one as being sufficient to keep God's covenant. The Lord's covenant hold the two together to the point where our relationship with God depends on the two co-existing, each giving life to the other. As we have seen, Jesus promises we will be justified in being called sons of the Father *if* we obey by loving our enemies.

This is why James, the brother of Jesus, taught the way he did in his letter, rejecting the idea that faith alone will justify anybody as God's son. Faith is never to be held in isolation, particularly when we are talking about justification, or being covenantally right with the Lord. It is an ironic tragedy that evangelicalism is built on the idea that faith alone is all that is necessary to be accepted as God's son. In James' day there were people who advocated the same thing. They taught that when it comes to acceptance before God, or justification, that faith alone is sufficient and good works should not enter into the discussion. But James powerfully rejects this idea as being "empty" or "foolish" (Jas. 2:20).

In order to reject this false understanding he takes us back to Genesis 22, to the example of Abraham's great act of obedience to the Lord's command to sacrifice his one and only son. As James explains it, "You see that his faith and his actions were working together, and his faith was made complete by what he did" (Jas. 2:22). Here we see that faith is not saving, or complete, until it is fulfilled with action, or obedience. What does James mean that faith is not complete without action?

James explains what he means, "And the Scripture was fulfilled that says, 'Abraham believed God, and it was credited to him as righteousness,' and he was called God's friend" (Jas. 2:23). God's estimation of Abraham as righteous in Genesis 15, when he believed, finds its fulfillment in Genesis 22, with his act of obedience to slay his son. Both are justifying moments in Abraham's life. In Genesis 22, Abraham is called God's friend *because he* obeyed God in faithfulness.

62

To be "called God's friend" is the same as to be justified, or reckoned to be in a right relationship with God (Is. 41:8; 2 Chr. 20:7).

As we have seen, on both occasions Abraham believed the Lord, and on both occasions he obeyed the Lord, keeping covenant with the Lord God. In Genesis 15, the Lord highlights faith, and in Genesis 22 he highlights obedience. In both Genesis 15, and in Genesis 22, Abraham was "reckoned right" with God. Obedience is always the necessary outworking of our faith, for justification, or the keeping of the covenant. This is why James closes this passage by saying, "You see that a person is justified by works and not by faith alone" (Jas. 2:24).

This is the main point that James wants us to get. We could say it this way, "You see that a person is *not* justified by faith alone." The logic is the same. But we must be clear; neither is James saying we are to add works to faith, as if these are two unrelated elements that need to be artificially joined. Rather, faith is the *means by which* we are to obey for justification. Faith serves the purpose of enabling obedience, as Paul puts it—an "obedience of faith" (Rom. 1:5;16:26). James' whole point is to keep faith and obedience tightly knit together when it comes to talking about justification, or the keeping of God's covenant. "What God has joined together, let man not separate."[13]

_____

13 The confession that we are "justified by faith alone" has become characterized through Luther and Calvin as the understanding of the covenant that keeps the church on the right track. This has become the "non-negotiable" doctrine of faithfulness, "the standing and falling church." The irony here is staggering. It appears that James would call such an assertion "foolish" and "empty." This faith alone view begs the question of why James would make what amounts to an unorthodox statement (that we are *not* justified by faith alone) in the defense of orthodoxy. Of course, it is argued that obedience is the *necessary consequence* of a saving faith, and that James is rejecting people who are teaching that works are not the necessary consequence of a saving faith. This is reflected in the well-known saying, "Faith alone justifies, but faith is never alone." However, this misrepresents James. James is saying that works make faith saving by completing faith itself. Works are not a necessary consequence as much as a part of faith that saves. This faith alone view goes radically astray as it divorces obedience from justification, the very thing that James is loath to do, and is the main point of his whole discussion.

12.

The Great Divorce Revisited

I have great regard for both Martin Luther and John Calvin as men of courage and faith, in the face of great opposition, to a move "back to the Scriptures." They broke with centuries of tradition, and traditional unquestioning allegiance to church authorities. What they accomplished in their great zeal for the Lord should never be minimized. However, these men and the traditions they spawned should never be enshrined with unquestioned magisterial authority. This was something that John Calvin humbly recognized as he wrote in his Institutes, "Above all, I must urge him (the reader) to have recourse to Scripture in order to weigh the testimonies that I adduce from it."[14] Here Calvin gives us a charge to go "back to the Scriptures" in order to weigh his own teachings. So if Calvin is wrong, and we follow his opinions, we are at fault for not weighing carefully enough his teaching with Holy Scripture.

Where Calvin, and Luther before him, were tragically wrong, was in rending the covenant into separate and unrelated compartments. The tight unity of the covenant that hold faith and obedience together for justification was pried apart. Faith was seen by Calvin as the part that relates to justification. Obedience comes next, as a necessary consequence of justifying faith, but has no causal relationship to it. This leads to a confession, or creed, which amounts to the opposite of what Scripture reveals. The Reformation heritage says in so many words, "You see we are justified by faith alone and not by works." Scripture says, "You see we are justified by works and not by faith alone."

For Calvin, the commands of Jesus and the Law of God become useful guides to holiness for the person who has already been "justified by faith alone." This understanding has had the effect of turning

---

14 Calvin, *Institutes*, Vol. 1. Westminster, 1960, 8.

Scripture on its head. Let me illustrate: Jesus' covenantal logic is reflected in Matthew 5:44,45 when He says "love your enemies that you may be sons of your Father in heaven." This is rendered very different, according to Calvin's faith alone teaching. For Calvin, those who have been justified by faith alone, and are established as God's sons, will love their enemies as a *necessary consequence* of being justified by faith alone. But for Jesus, being justified as "God's son" lies at the end of obedience, and the future promise of sonship is the motivating factor for that obedience. For Calvin, the declaration of sonship comes by "faith alone," and then the obedience of loving our enemies becomes a necessary consequence of being God's sons already. The problems here are obvious.

First, Jesus' future promise of sonship is depicted as to no longer be a future promise. Second, the promise of sonship is no longer dependent upon the command to love our enemies. The promise is torn away from the command. For Calvin, sonship is now attained without reference to the command at all, and can be had by faith in the promise alone. This, I contend, is a blatant mis-representation of the teaching of Scripture. This mis-representation strikes at the covenant God has made with mankind through Jesus Christ. Therefore, the consequences are nothing less than disastrous.

James represents faith and works as working together in the sense of being complimentary. But take note, he intends for us to understand that faith and works work together *for justification.* This is why he concludes by saying, "You see, a man is *justified by works* and not by faith alone" (Jas. 2:24). We cannot rip one away from the other *for justification.* James asserts this necessity by insisting to those who hold to faith alone for justification that faith alone is dead. "Faith by itself is dead," therefore it cannot justify anyone (Jas. 2:17). In separating faith from works for justification we kill faith.

In order to explain this, let's continue with Jesus' covenantal logic in Matthew 5:43-45. Jesus promises sonship for those who obey his command to "love your enemies." It is this promise that we are to embrace by faith. The object of faith is the future promise of being declared as God's son, and we obtain that promise by a life of faithfulness in loving our enemies. But Calvin's understanding that sonship is *not* a future promise but *only* present possession to be had by faith alone causes us to take our eyes off of the goal that Jesus Himself commands us to fix them on, which is our *future* declaration of sonship! Faith loses its proper Jesus-given focus.

We may say we have faith and believe in Jesus, but if we don't believe what Jesus told us to believe, then these words about faith and believing are empty. They have lost their biblical-covenantal content. Jesus has given us what to believe, but if we refuse what He has given us to believe, then faith, biblically considered, is dead. And when faith dies, then obedience cannot be sustained because it no longer has the will to live. When faith is dead, loving our enemies is a command that we have no power to obey, because the God -ordained motivation for obedience, which is faith in the promise of our future declaration of sonship, has just been torn away. John Calvin, in his commentary on Matthew, reflects this down-grade of what Jesus taught. Here is Calvin's explanation of Jesus' teaching:

> No-one wins this distinction for himself (sonship), no-one begins to be a son of God from the time he loves his enemies - but this is Scripture's normal way of speaking, to present the free gifts of God as a reward, by way of encouraging us to do the right thing.[15]

Notice Calvin acknowledges that Scripture's "normal way of speaking" is to present the gifts of God "as a reward." In other words, Calvin acknowledges that Scripture, in many places, presents what he considers to be by faith alone, *as if* it were obtained as a reward for good works. But of course this begs the question; why would God speak *as if* something is true when it isn't? Why would the Lord present the promise (sonship) *as* a reward for obedience when it is not? It seems far more likely to be true that Calvin's insists on faith alone *as if* this is the teaching of Scripture, when it is not. It is more likely that Calvin is at odds with Scripture, than Scripture is at odds with itself. But that is not all! We see the effect this has on Jesus' command for us to love our enemies. Calvin downgrades this from a command of necessity *for sonship,* as Jesus presents it, to a mere "encouragement for the sons of God to do the right thing." This teaching represents Jesus as playing motivational gamesmanship by speaking non-truths for a desired effect. May it never be! It is all too clear why Calvin must reason like this. He must uphold his faith alone teaching, even if it conflicts with the clear teaching of Scripture. It is beyond the scope of

---

15 Calvin, *Commentary on Matthew*, Baker, 1974,199.

this writing to delve into all the possible motivations that led John Calvin to reason in this way. But whatever the motivation, it is clear that the teachings of Calvin contrast with Jesus at this point. He not only clashed with Jesus, he also clashed with the apostle Paul.

Paul, in 1 Timothy 6, commands certain things of Timothy and of wealthy people in the church. Beginning in verse 17, Paul instructs Timothy to "command those who are rich in this present world not to be arrogant nor to put their hope in wealth, which is so uncertain, but to put their hope in God, who richly provides us with everything for our enjoyment." Note that this is not to be just an encouragement, or a friendly suggestion, but a command. He then goes on to describe what is at stake in keeping this command, "In this way they will lay up a treasure for themselves as a firm foundation for the coming age, *that they may take hold of the life that is truly life"* (6:19). But what does that mean? Does Paul mean a particular quality of life in heaven? Paul used the same phrase in earlier verses while exhorting Timothy toward faithfulness. He told him to "flee sin" and "take hold of the *eternal* life to which you were called" (6:11-12).

So we can understand from the prior context to "take hold of life" means to "take hold of eternal life" itself. Eternal life remains the future promise of "the coming age." How is it the rich in this age are to take hold of the promise of eternal life in "the coming age"? They are to take hold of eternal life *by* being generous and willing to share in this life! In other words, they are to "love their neighbor" who is in need. They are not to be like the wealthy man in Jesus' parable who hoarded his wealth to his own destruction, but was not "rich toward God" by loving others (Lk. 12:16-21). Once again, the covenantal structure is in view. The great promise and privilege is eternal life in "the coming age." The obligation is to love those in need in this age. It is by obeying "the command" to be generous that we will enjoy the privilege of the future promise.

The covenantal logic is crystal clear in Paul's commands for Timothy and the wealthy in the church. But, when we pick up Calvin's commentary on this section of Scripture, the covenantal clarity becomes unclear. Calvin's commitment to the faith alone doctrine muddies the waters of Paul's clear teaching. Calvin describes Paul as not laying the promise of eternal life before the wealthy. He represents Paul as meaning "they will obtain for themselves treasure in heaven" as a reward. So rather than Paul's assertion that heaven itself is taken hold of by being generous, Calvin changes this to treasures in heaven. However, this explanation fails to consider Paul's thoughts. Paul explicitly says that by being generous "they will lay up treasure for themselves as a firm foundation for the coming age, *so that they may take hold of the life that is truly life.*" Clearly, for Paul, life in the age to come is the treasure, and eternal life is the end result of being generous.

What is the motivation for Calvin to explain "taking hold of life" as being generous in order to get treasures in heaven, but not heaven itself? For Calvin, "heaven itself is attained through "the righteousness of faith" (faith alone) and the good works that Paul commands is to "be viewed as an appendix to it."[16] Calvin's prior commitment to faith alone leads him, by necessity, to change Paul's clear meaning. For Paul, being generous to those in need leads to "taking hold of eternal life." For Calvin, being generous to those in need becomes "an appendix" to saving faith, that alone justifies. For Calvin, if faith alone is true, then Paul simply can't mean that we take hold of eternal life *by* being willing to share with those in need.

The tragedy here is that God's saving and gracious covenant now becomes misrepresented at its most crucial point. The covenant is misrepresented at the point it is understood that "we take hold of eternal life." Nothing is more important than that! The reason that I spend so much time discussing Calvin's views on justification and its relation to obedience, is that evangelicalism as a whole swims in the stream of this theological perspective.

---

16 Calvin, *Commentary on 1 Timothy*, Baker, 1974, 83, "But after God has reconciled us to Himself by free grace, He accepts our services such as they are, and bestows on them a reward they do not deserve. Thus our reward does not depend upon considerations of merit, but on God's gracious acceptance, and is so far from being opposed to the righteousness of faith that it may be viewed as an appendix to it."

13.

The Gospel: Saved By Faithfulness to Christ Alone

What I have been contending for leads to some very important questions. If it is true that our contemporary views of God's covenant are off base, how did we arrive at such a tragic misunderstanding of the Bible? Is it really possible that so many could be wrong for so long, about something so important as God's will in saving mankind? Isn't this crucial truth of the Gospel so simple that a child can understand it? However, the most important question arises about all those passages that reject salvation by works; what do we do with those? These are important questions.

The first question concerning *how* we could misunderstand God's covenant so badly is a question that is too large for the scope of this book. That is like asking how it could be that a German nation could stand behind a ruler that was so patently evil as Adolf Hitler. That question will never be totally answered because so many social, cultural, religious and economic factors were involved. But in the case of Germany under Adolf Hitler, the facts remain. They *did* support his rule, as wrong as it was. And in the case of the Reformation doctrine of faith alone, that facts remain, the Reformers, and others *have misread crucial portions of Scripture*.

On the second question, we must recognize that the dark side of history is the story of men willfully misunderstanding God's covenant with mankind. The Reformation was a period of great progress in our understanding when "back to the Scriptures" became a core value, and a massive religious framework built on superstition and ignorance was thrown off. But we must remember that superstition and blatant false teaching had been accepted for several hundred years prior to Martin Luther and would continue to be accepted by many even after the

Reformation.

Is the Gospel a simple message that a child can understand? Yes, it is. But what we have here are competing simple messages. It is simple to believe the concept that the sun circles around the earth, but it is also simple to believe that the earth revolves around the sun. A child can understand either concept equally well, even though only one concept is the truth. It is possible to misread a simple truth, especially when you factor in the sinful human drive to suppress what is plain for all to see! Martin Luther recognized this in his day when he wrote,

> Let the Diatribe[17] now come and tell us how it is possible for one ordinary person to see what all these public figures, the chief men of all these ages, did not see! Even a schoolboy would conclude that this passage proves them to have been blind pretty often![18]

The last but most important question: What about those passages that reject works for salvation? Those passages have become bedrock texts for the Reformers in their insistence on justification by faith alone. But what we will clearly see, is that Paul was rejecting two specific viewpoints on good works when he rejected works for justification. It is crucial to see precisely what Paul was against in these passages, so we are able to discern the legitimate role works have for Paul in regard to justification.

The first passages the Reformers interpreted, as establishing their faith alone teaching, was Paul's vigorous insistence in many places that we are justified by faith and not by "works of the law" (Rom. 3:20, 28; 9:32; Gal. 2:16; 3:2, 5, 10, 12). The situation Paul and the apostles were facing is well-chronicled in Acts chapter 15. A council was held in order to decide what to do with the crisis of false teachers who were leading people astray. What were they teaching? Were they teaching a false gospel, that you must obey Jesus in order to be saved? No, they were teaching something else. They were not pointing to Christ at all, but away from Him. Acts 15:1 states, "Some men came down from Judea to Antioch and were teaching the brothers, 'Unless you are *circumcised, according to the custom taught by Moses,* you cannot be saved.' This brought Paul and Barnabas into sharp

---

17 Erasmus' writings against the doctrine of predestination.
18 Luther, Bondage of the Will. Revel, 1994, 173.

dispute with them."

This false teaching is described again in Acts 15:5, "Then some of the believers who belonged to the party of the Pharisees stood up and said, 'The Gentiles must be *circumcised and required to obey the law of Moses.*' The apostles and the elders met to consider this question." From this passage, we can gain an understanding of the false teaching that Paul so vigorously opposes in his letters. The false teachers wanted everyone to return to the Old Covenant, even after Jesus Himself had instituted the New Covenant. They were going against what Jesus had commanded. To retain the Old Covenant practices as mandatory for justification is to take the focus off Jesus, His commands and His promises.

To do this constitutes a denial of Christ, since He came to fulfill the Old Covenant and to establish the New Covenant (Mt. 5:17). Not only that, the Old Covenant was about Jesus Christ, and He is the fulfillment of the Old Covenant's office of High Priest (Heb. 7:23-26). He is the fulfillment of the Old Covenant's spotless lamb (Rev. 5:12). He is the fulfillment of the Old Covenant's temple of the living God (Jn. 2:20, 21). The Old Covenant contained mere shadows and symbols of the real thing, Jesus Christ (Col. 2:17). To turn back to the Old Covenant is tantamount to a denial of the reality, Jesus, the Messiah of the prophets, and fulfillment of the Old Covenant.

To put it another way, since the Old Covenant is about Jesus, to turn away from Jesus and to go back to the Old is, in reality, to deny and break the very purpose of the Old Covenant, which leads us to faith in Jesus (Gal. 3:24)![19] This is nothing less than a disastrous teaching that seeks to undermine the New Covenant with God and send people back under the curses of the Old Covenant.

One of my seminary professors presented this useful illustration of this sinful impulse to return to the Old Covenant. A young man goes away for a long period of time and his wife writes letters and send pictures to him. He sets the pictures of her up by his bedside table and remembers her with great fondness as he looks at her pictures. He, through the pictures, remembers her voice and wonderful times they have shared together. Finally, at long last, they are reunited. But as the

19 This reference to the law being a "custodian-male nursemaid- tutor" in Galatians 3:24 is not necessarily a negative one in the sense of being antithetical to faith. The following context speaks of the Old Covenant being for "children" who are under the supervision of a "custodian" which is the law, but when Christ comes we reach maturity and are no longer in need of the "tutor" services of the law.

days go by after being reunited, he ignores her and instead looks dreamily at the picture of her. He turns away from the real person as he continues his attachment to her picture. This would not only be very strange behavior; it would be a great offense to her! She would be jealous and angry about this misuse of her picture, and his lack of attention and devotion. Even though the picture was only meant to be used temporarily as a way to remind him of the real person, his attachment to the picture alone reveals a misplaced affection to some imaginary person, not the real person.

In the same way, a return to the Old Covenant is a turning away from the true and living Lord revealed in Christ, and a turning to what was only meant to be a temporary representation. The "circumcision group" was attempting to do nothing less than this. Just like the wife in the story would want to rip up the picture in jealous anger, so Paul expresses God's jealousy with his God-inspired words, "As for those agitators, I wish they would go the whole way and emasculate themselves" (Gal. 5:12)!

This is why Paul consistently and aggressively opposes these teachers who wish to return to the Old Covenant. But, this is the point that the Reformers missed; when Paul taught against "works of the law" for justification, he is resisting the false teaching that sends us back under the Old Covenant. We see this truth in Paul's letter to the Galatians. What did the false teachers insist on as a necessity for the church in Galatia? They were insisting on circumcision. This is why Paul would call them "the circumcision group" (Gal. 2:12). Notice what "works" Paul was vigorously rejecting;

> We who are Jews by birth and not 'Gentile sinners' know that a man is not justified by works *of the law,* but by faith in Jesus Christ. So we, too, have put our faith in Christ Jesus that we may be justified by faith in Christ and not by works *of the law,* because by works *of the law* no one will be justified (Gal. 2:15, 16).

At this point the Reformers fell into the ditch on the opposite side of the road. When they read this text, they understood Paul to mean rejecting good works in total, even the works that Jesus commands us to do. But this is not the works that Paul was rejecting. As we saw in Acts 15, the problem was a return to the "works of the law" or obeying Moses to be saved. We see that Paul could not mean works in total in his letter to the Galatians because he closes his letter by exhorting the church to obey Jesus *for eternal life*.

First he states, "Carry each other's burdens, and in this way you will fulfill the law of Christ" (6:2). Then he exhorts them to "not become weary in *doing good*, for at the proper time you will reap a harvest if we do not give up" (Gal. 6:9). What is the harvest that is to be reaped in doing good? The prior verse tells us. "The one who sows to please the Spirit, from the Spirit *will reap eternal life*" (Gal. 6:8). So the reaping of the harvest is equated with reaping eternal life, and it follows that we reap eternal life *by doing good*. What we see from the prior context, is that *doing good* in "carrying each other's burdens" is "fulfilling the law of Christ." It is clear Paul is rejecting "works of the law" given by Moses. It is equally clear what he is not rejecting the idea that we must do the works that Jesus commands us to do for eternal life. This is the important difference that the Reformers missed.

Paul's letter to the church in Galatia was a favorite for Luther. It is instructive for us to look at how Luther dealt with these closing verses which exhort the church to good works for eternal life. He recognizes the plain sense of Paul's teaching when he asks the question,

> Here rises a question, whether we deserve eternal life by our good works? For so Paul *seems*[20] to vouch in this place... Very necessary it is, after the example of Paul, to exhort the faithful to good works, that is, to exercise their faith by good works; for if they follow not faith, it is a manifest token that their faith is no true faith.[21]

Luther's reasoning is the same as what we saw with Calvin. Luther reasons that Paul *seems* to speak *as if* eternal life were dependent upon good works. Luther reasons that Paul wrote in this way because good works are crucial in order to verify true faith. In other words, good works are not a pre-requisite for eternal life as Paul *seems* to say, but they are simply a necessary consequence of having saving faith. In this section of Luther's commentary he refrains from going into great detail on how he interprets Paul's statements in this way, because he considers his comments on Paul's rejection of "works of the law" in

---

20 Italics is mine to highlight Luther's logic.
21 Luther, *Galatians Commentary*, Kregel, 1979, 370.

Galatians chapter 5 to be sufficient to prove his case. He maintains that Paul meant all works whatsoever. So here we see Luther's confusion of categories. He considers it impossible that Paul requires good works for eternal life in chapter 6 when he has already rejected "works of the law" in chapter 5. Apparently, Luther never considered the possibility that Paul was rejecting Old Covenant works in chapter 5, while affirming the necessity of New Covenant works in chapter 6.

The interpretation that Paul was rejecting a return to Old Covenant "works of the law" in his letters makes good sense of many of Paul's statements in which he maintains the necessity for good works, as follows:

"Circumcision is nothing and uncircumcision is nothing. Keeping God's commands is what counts" (1 Co. 7:19).

"For in Christ neither circumcision nor uncircumcision has any value. The only thing that counts is faith working through love" (Gal. 5:6).

"Neither circumcision nor uncircumcision means anything; what counts is a new creation. Peace and mercy to all who follow this rule" (Gal. 6:15,16).

There is a second sense in which Paul rejects works for salvation. He rejects the idea that God is a debtor to anyone, whether he is a Jew or a Gentile. No one is called into a relationship with God by a debt that God owes, but only by mercy. Paul was cutting the ground out from any possibility of our boasting about our salvation. In several places he does this by pointing out that the Lord called us out of sinful and disobedient lives. The Lord did not look down the corridors of time and see certain righteous people doing good works and decide to call them into a relationship with Him. This would give us a real cause for boasting. Our salvation would then be based on our working, *independent of God's gracious call.* This false understanding would make God's call dependent upon our pre-existent goodness. Rather, what we see is the Lord calling Abram *out of* idolatry, Matthew *from* his corrupt tax collector's booth, and Paul *out of* his murderous and idolatrous devotion to the Law of Moses. It is is clear that this was Paul's intent from the following passages;

76

God, who has saved us and called us to a holy life - not because of anything we have done but because of his own purpose and grace. This grace was given us in Christ Jesus before the beginning of time (2 Ti. 1:9).

Here is a trustworthy saying that deserves full acceptance: Christ Jesus came into the world to save sinners—of whom I am the worst. But for that very reason I was shown mercy so that in me, the worst of sinners, Christ Jesus might display his unlimited patience as an example for those who would believe and receive eternal life (1 Ti. 1:15,16).

All of us also lived among them at one time, gratifying the cravings of our sinful nature and following its desires and thoughts... But God... made us alive with Christ... For it is by grace you have been saved, through faith - and this not from yourselves, it is the gift of God - not by works, so that no one can boast (Eph. 2:3,4,8).

At one time we too were foolish, disobedient, deceived and enslaved by all kinds of passions and pleasures... But when the kindness and love of our Savior appeared, he saved us, not because of any righteous things we had done, but because of his mercy (Tit. 3:3,4,5).

Notice that, in all four of these important passages, Paul is referring to God's mercy in calling us to Himself, *out of* a place of sin and idolatry. His call into His covenant is not based on our doing good, because "all have sinned and fall short of the glory of God" (Rom. 3:23). When the Lord calls a man He calls him from a pool of sinners. But here we must be careful in our interpretation, so we stay out of the ditch the Reformers fell into. While it is true that Paul, Matthew and Abraham were "foolish, disobedient, deceived and enslaved by all kinds of passions and pleasures" *before* being graciously called into fellowship with the living God; it is *not* to say they were able to stay this way. Part and parcel with being called into a relationship with the Lord is the call to obey all that He says. The Lord calls us *out of* disobedience and *into* obedience; *out of* foolishness and *into* wisdom; *out of* slavery to sinful passions and pleasures, and *into* slavery to God; *out of* living for this world and the vain pursuits of this world, and *into* living for God, which will never be a vain pursuit; and He calls us *out of* faithlessness and *into* faithfulness.

For Calvin, Luther and the Reformation theology which followed, God's call *and* covenant is totally unconditional. He calls us to be His treasured possession by faith alone. For the Reformers, once we really understand the freeness of the Gospel's unconditional nature, we will be so grateful for this free gift that we will want to obey Him as a necessary consequence.[22] They are careful to assert that being God's treasured possession is not in any way dependent upon our obedience or good works, but good works will be the appendix or the necessary consequence of *really* being justified by faith alone. This is like saying that you give a child the whole house, everything in it is his, there is nothing he has to do in order to get it, it is given without *any* conditions. If the child *really* understands the freeness of the gift and that he doesn't deserve any of it, he will just want to cut the grass and do the dishes and clean out the kitty litter. Gratitude for the absolute free gift will propel obedience and good works. The good works done in gratitude will show that the child *really* understands how unconditional the gift of the whole house really is. Of course, real life does not work that way, and neither does the Lord's gracious covenant.

It is true that God's call comes to us freely and unconditionally. Abram, Matthew and Paul did not deserve to be called by God. But what they didn't deserve was the gracious call *out of allegiance* to sin and the world and the devil, and *into a covenantal allegiance* to the living God. It is the whole covenant that has been graciously offered and the whole covenant consists in promises for the future, commands for the present, and the historical accounts of God's faithfulness in the past. All is theirs and it has been given by mercy.

This truth is seen in Jesus' call of His disciples. He did not call them to Himself because of their good works. He also doesn't say to them, "I want you to understand that I have graciously called you into an unconditional covenant in which you are justified by faith alone. There is nothing you can *do* to have me not love you, *because* my love to you is by faith alone." Do you see the difference? This is the assertion of the Reformers and now evangelical theology in their wake.

---

22 Luther, "The Freedom of a Christian," *Martin Luther's Basic Theological Writings,* Fortress, 1989, 609, "This, as has been said above, is a necessary consequence on account of faith in Christ. So the heart learns to scoff at death and sin and say to the Apostle, 'O death, where is thy victory?'"

This is not the assertion of Jesus.

In John 14 and 15, Jesus makes abundantly clear that he has graciously called the twelve into a covenant which is conditional by definition, "Whoever has my commands and obeys them, he is the one who loves me. He who loves me will be loved by my Father, and I too will love him and show myself to him" (Jn. 14:21). "Remain in my love, *if* you obey my commands, you will remain in my love, just as I have obeyed my Father's commands and remain in His love" (Jn. 15:9b,10). We remain in Jesus' love by loving our brothers.

So Paul's point is that Jesus does not call us on the basis of good works, but He does call us out of the world and sin *for* good works as they have been covenantally mandated. *This is the crucial point: these good works that Jesus has called us to, are the good works that keep us in His love.* They must not be seen as just a necessary consequence, merely an appendix, or reduced to encouragements for holy living. It remains true that we live "on every word that comes from the mouth of God" (Deut. 8:3). We are Jesus' treasured possession as He has showed us his love, and at the same time we will be His treasured possession as we obey His commands to love our brothers, bless and not curse, show mercy, and even love our enemies.

Here Calvin stumbles. He cannot bring himself to say what Jesus says in John 15. When Jesus commands us to "remain in His love" in John 15:9, Calvin understands Jesus to mean that He is not demanding anything from us. To "remain in Jesus' love" is, for Calvin, an exhortation to continue to believe in Jesus' unconditional love, through faith alone.

> "Some expound this that Christ demands from His disciples love in return. Others are better, who take it actively as Christ's love. He wants us continually to enjoy the love with which he once embraced us and continually warns us to beware not to deprive ourselves of it."[23]

Jesus, in fact, is demanding love from the disciples in the form of obedience, and it is couldn't be clearer from Jesus' own words that remaining in Christ's love does *not* mean continue to continue in faith alone; it *is* a call to obedience of faith. Jesus is calling us to faith by His command to obey. As Dietrich Bonhoeffer put it,

23 Calvin, *Commentary on John,* Baker, 1974, 97.

The actual call of Jesus and the response of single-minded obedience have an irrevocable significance. By means of them Jesus calls people into an actual situation where faith is possible...because he knows that it is only through actual obedience that a man can be liberated to believe."[24]

We can illustrate it this way. If a person takes rock climbing lessons, one of the things the climber learns is to repel from the top. To repel, he has to lean back, while being suspended by a rope, and walk backwards down the cliff's face. The hardest part is getting started, actually taking that first step out over the edge. The teacher will tell the student to step out over and start repelling. The command has been given. It is not until the climber obeys the command to step, that faith in the rope, and the instructor exists. The command provides the occasion for faith! It is what the climber must *do* that makes faith necessary.

Jesus' command to us is a call for faith; to *believe* that Jesus *will love* us as we love Him, and love our brothers. Jesus is calling us to faith, to *believe* that He will forgive us as we forgive our brothers from the heart. Jesus is indeed calling us to faith, to *believe* that He will show us mercy as we show mercy to others. He is *not* calling us to faith alone. He is *not* calling us to believe that He forgives us, and is merciful to us, and loves us without regard for our behavior. That type of faith amounts to a faith other than what Jesus holds out for us, and another faith is belief in another message, and another message is in reality another gospel. Dr. C. van der Waal writes, "It is impossible to preach a gospel from which the covenant has been removed. It is impossible to speak of the kingship of God, without bringing the covenant into it. The Great King is the God of the covenant. His Royal Word is covenantal."[25]

Jesus gives us a whole host of things to believe, called promises. Then He gives us a whole host of commands. To believe in Jesus, is to believe all that He promised, and it is by believing in all that He promised, we are required to obey all He commanded. Never do we get even a hint that these are merely encouragements or appendixes to what really matters. It all really matters, every word that has proceeded from the mouth of our Savior. The good news is the invitation into this

---

24 Bonhoeffer, *The Cost of Discipleship*, 91-92.
25 van der Waal, *The Covenantal Gospel,* 175.

New Covenant that calls us *out of* darkness and *into* His wonderful light!

For many, this assertion will lead to an objection. They will resist the thought that to believe in Jesus is to believe all that He said and taught, because the Scriptures talk so powerfully about being justified by the blood of Jesus. If we are justified by the blood of Jesus, aren't we adding to the gospel if we say we must believe in something more than the death of Jesus for our sins? Indeed, it is preciously true that we are justified by the blood of Jesus. This is biblically beyond dispute.

The real question is; *"How* are we justified by the blood of Jesus?" The expert in the law, referred to in Luke 10, recited accurately the biblical fact that he was to love his neighbor. This begged a question. *Who* is his neighbor? That was the all-important question, because the answer to that question would determine whether or not he had loved his neighbor. It is one thing to recite the biblical fact that we are justified by the blood of Jesus. It is quite another to understand *how* we are justified by the blood of Jesus. Just like the answer to the lawyer's question of Luke 10, the answer to that question will determine if we actually are one of those justified by His blood!

14.

How We Are Justified By the Blood of Jesus

It is clear from Scripture that faith in Christ's finished work on the cross justifies us and reconciles us to God from the first moment of faith. This is how we can speak of having been redeemed in the past, and the reality of that redemption is celebrated in the present. This is clear from various Scripture passages:

"Therefore, having been justified by faith we have peace with God through our Lord Jesus Christ" (Rom. 5:1).

"...it was to prove at the present time his righteousness and that he is righteous and is justifying him who has faith in Jesus" (Rom. 3:26).

"In him we have redemption through his blood, the forgiveness of sins, according to the riches of his grace" (Eph. 1:7).

"You were redeemed from the empty way of life handed down to you from your forefathers...with the precious blood of Christ" (1Pet. 1:18-19).

When we refer to being justified by the blood of Christ, it is right and biblically beyond dispute to refer to our pardon being established by Jesus' finished work on the cross. Jesus takes our sins upon Himself and takes the Father's wrath against our sins and bears it so that we might be pardoned and escape wrath. This is what Paul refers to in Romans 5:9, "Therefore, being justified now by his blood..." The parallel to this statement is found in verse 10, "While being enemies we *were reconciled* to God by the death of his Son, much more, *while being reconciled,* shall we be saved by his life." The cross of Jesus is the place of our pardon, where the guilt of our sins are atoned for. Christ's death and resurrection stand as a central moment of God's redemptive work in the New Covenant just as the Exodus was the central moment of God's redemptive work in the Old Covenant.

However, what we must also see is that Christ's death and resurrection is not ultimate in God's scheme of redemption. Jesus Christ's atoning work on the cross, while essential to our salvation, is not end of our redemption, just as the deliverance from Egypt and the crossing of the Red Sea was not the end of Israel's redemption. Christ's death and resurrection becomes the all-sufficient fountain from which our redemption springs; this is central to our faith. However, Christ's death and resurrection was, and is, the essential *means* by and through which God's *ends* for our redemption is accomplished. The end or the goal of Christ's death and resurrection is our future vindication or justification at the judgment seat of God.

It is striking to note that nowhere in Scripture is the final justification at the last judgment seen as accomplished by God's people "claiming the blood of Jesus." Nowhere in Scripture do you see the ground of a person's declaration of innocence at the judgment of God being a proper confession of Jesus' finished work on the cross, despite being a foundational assumption in contemporary evangelicalism. It is assumed that at the judgment, the only basis of being able to enter eternal life is a proper confession of Jesus' substitutionary atonement. The danger this presents to us is obvious. If popular evangelical preaching and teaching is misguided on this point, then thousands will be entering the tribunal of the Lord being profoundly ill- equipped for that great day. There will be thousands of confessions that are accurate enough concerning the central means by which God redeems the world, namely Christ's death and resurrection. But it is apparent from Scripture that God's judgment will *not* be according to a proper recitation of God's means. The fact to be evaluated on that great day will be whether the means of God's redemption, namely the death and resurrection of Jesus, will have found its constituted end, or goal in a person's life. It will be on that basis that justification at the judgment seat of God will occur.

I want to pause to acknowledge that many of my evangelical brethren will be catching their breath at this moment and assume that I have just blasphemed the glorious finished work of the cross of Christ. I would implore you to withhold judgment, because I believe the opposite to be true. The truth is, if we stop at Christ's work on the cross, and go no further to the goal of Christ's redemption, then the glory of God through Christ cannot, and will not, be shown forth in the way that God has intended. But first we must take a closer look at the logic of God's covenantal Word in this regard. We must examine the grammar of Scripture that shows Christ's death and resurrection to be the means to God's glorious ends.

The most useful aspect of grammar that I was taught in Seminary, is how conjunctions that join sentences and phrases communicate the author's logic for a particular argument. For example, note the following:

"And he died for all, *in order that* the ones living should no longer live for themselves but for him who died for them and rose again" (2 Co. 5:15).

"For our sake he him who had no sin to be sin for us, *in order that* we might become the righteousness of God" (2 Co. 5:21).

"He himself bore our sins in his body on the tree, *in order that* we might die to sin and live for righteousness" (1 Pet. 2:24).

"...sending his own Son in the likeness of sinful flesh and for sin, he condemned sin in the flesh, *in order that* the just requirements of the law might be fulfilled in us, who walk not according to the flesh but according to the Spirit" (Rom. 8:3b-4).

These verses reveal a logic of means and ends. The conjunction *in order that* reveals this logical relationship. The first half of the sentence is the "means." The second half indicates the "ends" for which the means occurs. In other words, the means occurs for the express purpose of accomplishing the ends. If I say, "I went to the store *in order that* I might buy some bread," then the purpose of going to the store was to buy bread. The act of going to the store is the means by which the end occurs. The point is the buying of the bread.

The same logic is used in our passages; Jesus' death is the means by which the people live for God. The end, or goal of Christ's death, is people living for God and dying to sin. The emphasis is the goal, which is living for God and not for sin. From the example, the *means* is going to the store. Bread is bought *by means of* going to the store. The goal is to buy the bread. The trip would not be seen as complete unless the purchase of bread had occurred. Only on the basis of bread being purchased would the trip to the store be viewed as successful, because the trip to the store itself was not the goal. The trip to the store was simply the means (though no doubt absolutely necessary) by which the end of purchasing bread was accomplished.

According to Paul's reasoning, *only on the basis of a life lived for God and not for sin* would Christ's necessary sacrifice on the cross be seen as effective. A person, according to our example, would be judged as having a successful trip to the store on the basis of bread brought home. The ends had been accomplished. In the same way, only on the basis of a life lived for God in pursuit of righteousness and dying to sin would a person be judged as manifesting the ends for which is the purpose of Christ's death.

This is why the future vindication is not according to a proper recitation of God's means, but is a demonstration of the ends being accomplished:

"I say to you, on the day of judgment men will render account for every careless word they utter; for by your words shall be your justification, and by your words shall be your condemnation" (Mt. 12:37).

"Come, O blessed of my Father, inherit the kingdom prepared for you from the foundation of the world; for I was hungry and you gave me food, I was thirsty and you gave me drink, I was a stranger and you welcomed me, I was a naked and you clothed me, I was sick and you visited me, I was in prison and you came to visit me" (Mt. 25:34-36).

"For it is not the hearers of the law who are righteous before God, but the doers of the law who will be justified" (Rom. 2:13).

"Speak and act as those who are going to be judged by the law that gives freedom, because judgment without mercy will be shown to anyone who has not been merciful. Mercy triumphs over judgment" (Jas. 2:12,13)!

"So we make it our goal to please him, whether we are at home in the body or away from it. For we must all appear before the judgment seat of Christ, that each one receive what is due him for the things done while in the body, whether good or bad" (2 Co. 5:9,10).

"Since you call on a Father who judges each man's work impartially, live your lives here in reverent fear" (1 Pet. 1:17).

"Judge me O Lord, according to my righteousness, according to my integrity, O Most High" (Ps. 7:8).

These passages refer to a future justification which will find its basis in our behavior. How do we reconcile such statements with the awesome and wonderful truth of Jesus' death on the cross for our sake? How can we reconcile the fact that Scripture testifies to Christ's justifying blood, and our justifying works? It is here that evangelicalism become fraught with confusion. Some evangelicals will say, "Oh, all the statements that speak about justifying works are part of the Old Testament way of doing things, that is how someone was saved in the Old Testament." But what about all those New Testament statements about being justified by words and deeds?

Others will say, "These statements are hypothetical, that these passages only speak about what is theoretically possible in a sinless world, *not* what is really possible." But do we dare to suppose this, when every indication is that Jesus and his apostles meant what they said, and were not speaking hypothetically? The danger in both of these solutions is that we end up believing we can ignore these passages because we know that Jesus "did it all" at the cross. When we come to the great day of judgment we "plead the blood of Jesus." But how do we reconcile such an idea with the passages we have just read?

The reconciliation of Christ's atoning death and our future justification by our behavior, is found in the Bible. It is found in placing Christ's death and resurrection in their proper place in God's redemptive purposes. Jesus' death and resurrection is the means by which our Father accomplishes His ends. The goal or end of Jesus' work on the cross is the creation of brothers and sisters who are just like Him. It is Christ's death and resurrection that makes this possible. But, the goal of Christ's death is our being raised to "newness of life." It is from this "newness of life" that we will be declared to be God's children. Now we can see how these passages can speak about being judged according to works *without* negating Jesus' death for our sake.

These passages are announcing the accomplished goal, or the end of Jesus' death and resurrection.

From this logic, it become clear why future justification finds its basis in our works, and *not* in pleading Christ's blood on our behalf. To plead Christ's blood alone at the judgment will be like coming back from the store empty handed and saying, "No, I don't have bread, but I went to the store!" The response would be, "That is not the point, the point of going to the store was to get bread!" To plead Christ's blood and not anything I have done at the judgment sounds humble enough, but it denies the express purpose of Christ's death - that is a life lived for God. If we deny the purpose of Christ's death, then we in effect deny Christ, and no amount of "pleading the blood" will suffice.

15.

How We Are Sanctified by the Blood of Jesus

Our justification by the blood of Christ is accomplished in the first moment of faith, but only with an eye toward a lifetime of consequent acts of faith expressed in repentance and confession. Our life under the cross is itself transformative as we repent, that is, turn from sin to righteousness. In fact, we are cleansed not by an empty profession of sin, but in the context of our intention to turn from sin to obedience. This dynamic is reflected in Isaiah 55:6,7, "Seek the Lord while he may be found; call on him while he is near. Let the wicked forsake his way and the evil man his thoughts. Let him turn to the Lord, and he will have mercy on him, and our God will freely pardon."

In this passage we can see that "turning to the Lord" is parallel with "forsaking evil ways and thoughts." In other words, "forsaking evil ways and thoughts" is to "turn to the Lord." Turning to the Lord cannot be reduced to confessing sin, but must also include an intention to do God's will, the act of forsaking. The result of this "turning to the Lord" in order to do God's will is that God will have mercy and "freely pardon" sins that have been committed. So the gift of God's free pardon is given in the context of a sinner resolving to forsake his sin and do God's will. This, for Isaiah, does not compromise the freeness of the pardon. In the context of repentance, which is a turning from sin to God, the Lord does not require payment for past sins, they are covered freely and mercy is received.

If the intention to turn from sin does not exist, then confession becomes reduced to a justification of sin rather than a justification of the sinner. Understanding that our justification depends on an on-going commitment to turn away from sin, opens us up to the possibility of a real and present knowledge, and an assurance of our justification. We are not left with a mere reflection about the validity of a transaction that took place in the past, but can hear the very real word of pardon *today* (2 Co. 6:1). This blessing was understood by the puritan theologian Jonathan Edwards and needs to be re-emphasized in our day.

> And then to suppose that no after acts of faith are concerned in the business of justification, and so that it is not proper for any ever to seek justification by such acts, would be forever to cut off those Christians that are doubtful concerning their first act of faith, from the joy and peace of believing. As the business of justifying faith is to obtain pardon and peace with God, by looking to God, and by trusting him for these blessings... The proper remedy (for those who doubt their first act of faith) is now by faith to look to God in Christ for these blessings.[26]

As Edwards recognized, this biblical reality of a present justification as we live under the cross daily would not serve to undermine the joy and wonderful assurance of believing. Rather, we would be restored, in the present joy of our salvation, hearing God's word of pardon and life-giving command to pursue His ways, as the freeing word of the gospel (Ps. 51:12). In order to illustrate this point, I will use a pastoral counseling anecdote to put flesh and bones on this biblical perspective.[27]

A young woman came into my office seeking counsel concerning anxiety she was feeling in regard to Jesus' acceptance of her. She related that she had a hard time knowing that she was truly forgiven. She prayed continually for God to help her and knew that Jesus had died for her sins, yet He seemed distant to her and she lacked assurance of her salvation. After asking many questions about her life, she revealed that she and her mother were having a difficult time. She felt as though her mother was not treating her fairly. and was even being somewhat abusive in her language. I inquired into how she responded to her mother's injustice, and she told me that they had shouting matches, and there were times when she slammed the door in her mother's face. This shed new and important light on her situation. I proceeded to define the distinction between her mother's behavior and her own. I did not want to justify her mother if she was indeed

---

26 Edwards, *The Works of Jonathan Edwards*, Vol. 1, Banner of Truth, 1995, 643.
27 Details have changed in order to not compromise confidentiality.

behaving the way that she was being portrayed. However, what this young woman needed to know was that she was not responsible for her mother's sin, but that she was only responsible for her own.

The Bible is clear that we are to honor our parents, and there are no exceptions to this commandment. Jesus has given this woman a command to honor her mother. This command is not dependent on her mother acting in godly ways. Part of the Christian calling is to bear the sin of others patiently, and to not fight wrath with wrath, or evil with evil. In fact, this is the very definition of bearing our crosses (1 Pet. 4:12-19). The young woman was refusing to carry her cross, and rather than overcoming evil with good, she was being overcome with evil (Rom. 12:21). It became clear *why* she was wrestling with assurance of her salvation, even though she knew that Jesus died for her sins. She was wrestling with her assurance for very good reasons. Biblical assurance comes from obedience to Jesus' commands, *not only* a recitation of the facts of Jesus' death on the cross for our sake (1 Jn. 2:3; 3:18-20).

The outcome of the counseling was for her to ask two people for forgiveness. First, she must be reconciled to her mother by asking her for forgiveness for not honoring her the way a daughter should. She must pursue peace with her mother to the degree that the peaceful results would depend upon her (Rom. 5:18). Then, she must go to God and repent of her sin of rebellion against His commands (Mt. 5:23, 24; 7:12). Then, she was reassured that God will draw close to her with His sweet assurance as she walks in His ways in repentance (Jas. 4:7-10). She will know His forgiveness in her repentance and in her renewed resolve to honor her mother. I also sympathized with the difficulty of seeking forgiveness from those who had wronged her and not repented, but for her to remember that she was not responsible for the acts or omissions of others. Loving those who wrong us is probably the most difficult thing Jesus commands us to do. Yet, He is asking nothing of us that He has not already done for us at the cross, and this is the paradoxical path to experiencing profound joy and the sweet assurance of our faith (Ac. 5:41; Rom. 5:3; Jas. 1:2-4).

This, I believe, is the way to experience biblical assurance. Otherwise, if assurance is obtained just by a recitation of what Jesus did for me on the cross, without repentance, and without turning to righteousness, all that we have left is the justification of sin, and continuing a life of sin. Without repentance, we become hardened, deceived and in reality, unforgiven and condemned, because we are denying Jesus as our Lord and Savior. This is the very teaching that Jude warned us about. "They are godless men, who change the grace of our God into a license for immorality and deny Jesus Christ our only Sovereign and Lord" (Jude v. 4b). The imperative of obeying the gospel must be pressed upon God's people (1 Pet. 4:17; 2 Th. 1:8).

It is a deficient gospel that calls us to simply reflect on a past transaction, of a redemption accomplished "at the cross," and to conjure up feelings of gratitude that are supposed to make us want to love our enemies, while at the same time being told our own forgiveness has nothing to do with the obedience of loving our enemies. We are told, "If we truly feel the forgiveness of Jesus that has been accomplished, then we will really want to go out today and love those who rub our faces in the dirt." This is a weak message that only respects one part of God's Word to us, and for us, and will by necessity produce weak and worldly Christians. The whole truth includes gratitude for sure, but it also connects our *present* forgiveness, our *present* reconciliation, our *present* salvation, and our *present* cleansing, with a resolve to forgive *now*, be reconciled to our brother *today*, and love our enemies *in the present*. In short, to obey Jesus Christ by taking up our own crosses *daily*. As we do so, we have the very real and present experience of assured peace with our Lord.

The practical reality of this distortion is that sins in the present become *justified* because of a perceived once for all transaction that has taken place. Our hearts become hard and our consciences become appeased with the false idea that "there is nothing more for us to do." This is not a reflection of the covenantal life that God requires, but is a disastrous perversion of it. The fear of the Lord, which is biblically portrayed as a healthy and life-giving reality, becomes drained of its sanctifying and repentance producing force. "There is no fear of God" becomes a virtue of having a distorted doctrine of grace and faith alone.

Repentance and confession implies a turning away from sin, to righteousness. A life lived under the cross is not simply hearing a word of pardon; it is hearing a word of pardon in the context of a pursuit of holiness. This reality is reflected in the Lord's Prayer, "Forgive us our sins, for we also forgive everyone who sins against us" (Lk. 11:4). The context in which sin is forgiven, is the one in which a resolution to follow Jesus in forgiving those who sin against me, exists. This is where we see the cross producing a righteous life, mercy is received only if mercy is given. James testifies in James 2:12,13, "mercy triumphs over judgment" only when we are merciful. To miss this is to miss something absolutely central to the Christian faith. The gift to us is *both* in the mercy received, *and* in our opportunity to bestow mercy. This is where a tragic division has occurred. The gift is not just the reception of pardon and *not* the command to pardon others. For us to pardon others and to bestow mercy is a gracious call and a gift! It is a gracious call to be healed of a hellish, bitter and resentful disposition that destroys our souls. And it is only in the context of this repentance that we can turn to the righteousness in which we are cleansed from our sin. The cross produces a pardoned *and* righteous people; this is the gift of God (Rom. 6:19-23). This is how Peter, John and the writer of Hebrews can speak about being sprinkled by the blood of Jesus *after* obeying Him.

"To those who are elect exiles... for obedience to Jesus Christ and for sprinkling with his blood" (1 Pet. 1:2).

"But if we walk in the light as he is in the light, we have fellowship with one another and the blood of Jesus his Son cleanses us from all sin" (1 Jn. 1:7).

"He became the source of eternal salvation for all who obey him" (Heb. 4:8).

These passages are nonsense unless we are able to understand Christ's cleansing blood as not just something that lies in the past, but also is a future reality to be obtained by the obedience of faith. This is also reflected by numerous passages that speak about a future salvation or justification. The covenant makes sense of this, as we, like the saints of old, are striving to be God's "treasured possession." In the following chapter, I will present a person who was striving for that prized declaration of sonship. That person will be the Apostle Paul himself.

16.

The Apostle Paul, Pressing On to the Goal of Eternal Life

The Apostle Paul understood his relationship with the Lord to be a covenantal one in which certain conditions had to be met. He understood the commands from Jesus to be more than encouragements for godly living, and a necessary consequence of being justified by faith alone. Eternal life itself hung in the balance for God's apostle. Blessings and curses had been laid before Paul and he was bound and determined to gain the blessings.

Prior to 1 Corinthians 9:23, Paul described his mission as a commission to proclaim the gospel, to be a herald of the good news of the New Covenant for all peoples. Then in verse 23 he relates to the Corinthians the reason he is diligent to carry out his mission. "I do all on account of the gospel, in order that I may be its fellow partaker." Paul understood his mission as a means by which he, himself, would be a sharer in the benefits of the gospel.

This statement needs further clarification. Is this a reference to his own salvation, or is it a reference to a future enjoyment that is above and beyond salvation, like increasing rewards in heaven? The language of verse 23 is vague because of its brevity, therefore it could be taken either way. However, Paul's reasoning steers us in just one direction.

He asks a question that is meant to shed light on what he had just written, "Do you not know that in a race all the runners compete, but only one receives the prize? So run in order that you obtain it." (v. 24) But what is "it"? In verse 24 we see that "it" refers to "the prize." But this still begs the question of the meaning of "the prize." Is it a reference to rewards in heaven, or heaven itself? Verse 25 provides the answer. Paul relates that the athlete exercises self control in order to get a "perishable crown," but we do it to get one that is "imperishable." What does Paul now mean by an imperishable crown?

Jesus Himself can help us with this, because in Revelation 2:10 He mentions the "crown of life"; a metaphor for eternal life itself. This is clearly Jesus' intention in Revelation 2:10, because the alternative to receiving the crown of life is the "second death" of hell. It makes the most sense to understand Jesus' crown of life to be Paul's imperishable crown, which represents eternal life. So as we use Scripture to interpret Scripture we are able to discern the prize to be eternal life itself. The imperishable crown to be gained is the crown of life and *not* hell as the alternative.

Paul then describes how "he beats his body and makes it his slave so that... I myself will not be disqualified for the prize" (1 Co. 9:27). So Paul's concern is that he, after preaching to others, will not fail to obtain eternal life, which we now know is the prize. This interpretation is further confirmed by what Paul understands to be the alternative to gaining the prize. The NIV translates Paul's concern to be a concern about being "disqualified for the prize." The Greek word translated as "disqualified" occurs five other times in the New Testament, and every time it deals with a person being rejected by God (Rom. 1:28; 2 Co. 13:5-7; 2 Ti. 3:8; Tit. 1:6; Heb. 6:8). Hebrews 6:8 reads, "But if it bears thorns and thistles, it is *disqualified* and near to being cursed; its end is to be burned." All the evidence points to the fact that Paul's concern for himself was not about losing rewards in heaven, it was much more serious than that, his concern was for reaching the prize, the imperishable crown, which is heaven itself.

But how did Paul see himself being "qualified" for the prize of eternal life? Was it by maintaining an ongoing understanding of Jesus' unconditional love for him based on faith alone? Clearly not. He wrote that he "beats his body and makes it his slave" so that he might *not* be disqualified for the prize. He is building off his athlete analogy where "self control" was the key point. An athlete exercises self control in diet and exercise so he can win the prize. Paul understood that it was necessary for him to exercise self control, not with diet and exercise, but with sin. He must not let sin be his master, but like Cain was commanded by God, he must master it. He must be a slave to righteousness and not to sin.

So Paul's fear was that after preaching the necessity for self control to the churches, he personally would fail to exercise it and be rejected by God. Paul was motivated by a covenantal fear of the Lord. He knew the blessings and the curses that were laid out before him, and because he desired God more than anything, he would fight hard for the prize in the good fight of the faith. This all sheds light on what Paul means in verse 23 by "becoming all things to all men, in order that I may be a fellow partaker" of the gospel. He means nothing less than partaking in the salvation that the gospel offers.

We also find Paul writing similar teachings in his letter to the church in Philippi. Philippians 3:7-14 reveals a pronounced tension between Paul's present experience of "knowing Christ" and what is to be obtained in the future. Paul relates how he "counts everything as loss because of the surpassing worth of knowing Christ Jesus my Lord" (v. 8a). The *knowing* is clearly a present reality. He knows Jesus, and this is further emphasized by Paul's affectionate reference to Jesus as *my* Lord. With this established in the first section, Paul proceeds with the second section of verse 8 by presenting a future reality. Paul has lost all things and even considers them rubbish, "in order that I may gain Christ and be found in Him..." Once more Paul employs a verb form, which carries the sense of a future-uncertain, yet hoped-for reality. "That I *may gain* Christ and *be found* in Him" (v. 8b).

Paul has left behind all his former social, religious and economic advantages in order that he *may gain* Christ, or, that he *may be found* in Christ. This entails a great deal of suffering that Paul considers to be a necessary exercise in cross-bearing. It is for him a personal experience of Christ's sufferings, "becoming like him in His death," and the result for him will be the same result that was for Jesus. Jesus attained to the resurrection by His suffering while obeying the Father. In the same way, Paul is to attain to the resurrection by his suffering while obeying Jesus.

But just as the promise of Jesus' resurrection lay before Him during His earthly ministry, and was no doubt a source of great comfort for Him (Heb. 12:1-3), so the promise of Paul's resurrection lay before him as his inspiration to press on. "Becoming like Him in His death, that *if possible* I *may attain* to the resurrection from the dead" (v. 11). The future, not yet attained, is the emphasis here. Paul expresses his hope "that I *may attain*," and this future hope that has not yet been attained is emphasized with the introduction of his statement with his insertion of *"if possible."*

You get a palpable sense of Paul's leaning forward, to the

future, and this sense is fanned into flames in verses 12-14. Paul has "not already attained all this or am already perfect." Paul has not already "gained Christ," and he does not already "know Christ" in the way in which he hopes to know Him at the resurrection. Verse 12 reveals this sense of covenantal tension in which Paul is already "knowing Christ Jesus my Lord" and yet hoping to "know Christ" and to be "found in Him." Paul "presses on that I *may* grasp [Him], because I *was grasped* by Christ Jesus." In verse 13, Paul emphasizes his contingent position when he writes, "Brothers, I do not consider myself to have taken hold [of Him]." So what does Paul do? He forgets what is behind and presses forward "according to the goal, to the prize of the upward call of God in Christ Jesus" (v.14). What is the prize? Paul here describes it here as the "upward call." Once again, it is the prize *of* the upward call or in other words, eternal life. Eternal life is entered by means of the resurrection from the dead, to be raised to life. So it is clear, that in these passages, while Paul has been grasped by Christ and knows him, it is also no less true that he sees himself as needing to "press on" to take hold of nothing less than eternal life.

This should all sound familiar. Just as Israel, at Mount Sinai, was already the Lord's treasured possession, Israel needed be faithful to the Lord by keeping His commands, so that they might continue to be the Lord's treasured possession. Paul, too, was in covenant with the Lord. He has been grasped by Christ and called into a relationship with Him. Now Paul was to press on in faithfulness to his Lord, and be willing to suffer like Jesus did, in order to remain as Jesus' treasured possession.

The apostle Paul had no knowledge of faith alone as a way in which this was done. This was not what he believed about his own life, let alone what he taught others. He had to suffer for Jesus, and he had to suffer because he had to obey. As he wrote in Romans 2:7, "To those who by persistence in doing good seek glory, honor and immortality, he will give eternal life."

17.

Where Do We Go From Here?

This work has been an attempt to raise awareness of the theological challenge in which we find ourselves, and the challenge is a great one. We evangelicals live in the midst of a stream of thought and faith that is held most dearly. Faith alone is held more or less self-consciously by evangelicals as the very cornerstone of evangelical orthodoxy. To be faithful to Jesus, in the main, is understood to mean holding to the doctrine of justification by faith alone. What makes matters worse, is the commonly held assumption that the only option to the doctrine of faith alone is a pursuit of "works righteousness" of the type that Paul rejects and Roman Catholicism endorses. This leads to irrational fears that to abandon faith alone will lead to a life of futile attempts to earn our way to heaven. These are seen to be the only two choices, hence we are subject of a logical fallacy, the fallacy of the excluded middle.

For evangelicals we are either justified by faith alone *or* by works. For Catholics we are justified by works the church directs us to do, as they are added to the things the church tells us to believe. These are the belief-ditches that lie on either side of "the way of righteousness" that Isaiah prophesied so powerfully about (Is. 26:7, 8; 35:8-10). The way of righteousness leading to the Kingdom of God is the path of God's commands in Scripture which are kept by faith. The excluded middle is not a mediating position between evangelicals and Catholics; it is the only way, and the only truth, and the only life, and Jesus guarantees that only a few will find it. Of course evangelicals and Catholics alike both strongly believe they are on this narrow way. These convictions are emotionally held and makes careful biblical reasoning very difficult, but careful biblical reasoning is the only way to know the truth about this way of righteousness.

This makes our position a difficult one indeed. But the truth must be told. We can't imagine the difficulty of a first century Jew proclaiming that someone who had been publicly crucified in a shameful way, is now sitting at the right hand of the Father ruling the world! God's glory shines through even more brightly in very dark times, and we have entered our own modern dark age. The dark age in religion was characterized by biblical ignorance and superstition, which work hand in hand. Not to understand the Scriptures is to be ripe for all kinds of aberrant beliefs and practices. Many of Roman Catholicism's current and cherished beliefs have grown out of such ignorance of the Scriptures.

We live in a day, however, in which a new darkness has fallen over Christendom. It is a darkness that has been born from ignorance just as the old darkness was. The old darkness was produced by an ignorance due to the lack of understanding of biblical revelation, by priest as well as by lay person. The fundamental reason was that the Sacraments were seen as *the* way in which we relate to God. Therefore, it follows that according to this view, knowing the Scriptures was at worst, not necessary, and at best, of a secondary concern. This, of course, was and is, theologically misguided. This error resulted in spiritual death and deprivation of a magnitude that is hard to even comprehend.

But the truth is, we live in a new darkness, a new dark age within evangelicalism, in which we are experiencing a spiritual death and deprivation of our own.[28] The new darkness is also born from ignorance of God's revealed will, and this ignorance is due to being theologically misguided. We, as evangelicals, are not misguided in the same way, for sure; we have liberated ourselves from the "Babylonian captivity" of Sacramental slavery. However, in the process, we have run into the arms of another slave master.

The very discovery of Luther and Calvin that led to their liberation from Rome resulted in an unholy alliance with the one who Paul most sternly warned us about in his second letter to the Thessalonians. Luther, while casting off the chains of Roman Catholic works righteousness, having to do with a whole host of unbiblical remedies for sin, bravely announced that not only was the Pope his enemy, but so was Moses. Moses, according to the reformer, is the

---

28 Dr. David Wells writes compellingly about this present reality in his three volume series entitled, *No Place for Truth, God in the Wasteland,* and *Losing Our Virtue.*

"hangman," the "minister of death." Luther, in his loathing of Roman Catholic demands, now loathed all demands whatsoever where justification is concerned. Demands, in the form of biblical commands, were seen as condemning words, and therefore Luther's enemy, to be renounced in the name of freedom. He would say in his *Table Talk*, "I will have none of Moses with his law, for he is an enemy to my Lord and Saviour Christ. If Moses will go to law with me, I will give him his dispatch, and say: Here stands Christ."[29] On another occasion he said,

> Moses with his law is most terrible; there never was any equal to him in perplexing, affrighting, tyrannizing, threatening, preaching, and thundering; for he lays sharp hold on the conscience, and fearfully works it, but all by God's express command. When we are affrighted, feeling our sins, God's wrath and judgments, most certainly, in the law is no justification; therein is nothing celestial and divine, but 'tis altogether of the world, which world is the kingdom of the devil.[30]

Conversely, Jesus is depicted as one who does not threaten but gently cajoles His already justified people. "By this we see that he forces not, but teaches amicably, saying: 'Blessed are the poor,' etc., 'Come to me all ye that are weary and heavy laden,' etc. And the apostles use the words: 'I admonish,' 'I exhort,' 'I pray,' etc.; so that we see in every place that the gospel is not a lawbook, but a mild preaching of Christ's merits..."[31] Luther seems to have forgotten that the Law of Moses exhorted faith in the God who is a "compassionate and gracious God, slow to anger, abounding in love and faithfulness, maintaining love to thousands, and forgiving wickedness, rebellion and sin" (Ex. 34:6). He seems to have forgotten that Jesus threatened his believing disciples with the torments of hell when he promised them, "This is how my heavenly Father will treat each of you unless you forgive your brother from your heart" (Mt. 12:35).

Luther divided law from gospel, Moses from Jesus and command from promise. Luther's great discovery that set him free from Rome, had the tragic effect of setting us free from Jesus and His New

---

29 William Hazlitt, *The Table Talk of Martin Luther,* Bell, 1875, 221.
30 *Table Talk,* 220.
31 *Table Talk,* 227.

Covenant. We evangelicals proudly assert that we are free to eat meat on Friday, and divorce at the same rate as the rest of the world. We crawled out of the muddy ditch on one side, and in our wild joy of new-found freedom, have blindly stumbled into the ditch on the other. It is a different ditch to be sure, but it is still a ditch. It is not the firm footing of the road which is the Way. The problem for us now is that we like our ditch. We even call our ditch old paths of orthodoxy just as they do in the ditch on the other side of the road.

We have escaped from papal captivity, for that we must be grateful. But we must not be so grateful that we fail to hear Jesus above the din of evangelical faith alone orthodoxy. The freedom of the faith alone evangelical is no freedom at all, but an invitation to slavery to sin, and that with an appeased conscience. Assurance of salvation is a prime selling point of the faith alone doctrine. We are frightened by the assertion that if we abandon faith alone we will have no assurance of God's acceptance. The clear conscience and assurance of the "faith alone' evangelical type hardens us to the sin we all know is wrong, but have no power to resist. We have no power to resist sin because, according to the faith alone doctrine, we have no real need to. This results in having a "form of godliness, but denying it's power" (2 Tim. 3:5).

The problem is that the kingdom of God is not about mere talk, but it is about power. Paul warned us of one who would come. He would be the "man of lawlessness" (2 Thess. 2:3). He would be one who would come as an angel of light and in the name of the Lord, proclaiming salvation and freedom from God's law. The man of lawlessness is indeed free from God's law and wants you to be free too, and like him, become a slave to sin, heading for death. He will preach fierce sermons of old path orthodoxy against false teachers who dare to obscure his counsel with heretical notions of obedience, repentance and covenant faithfulness. He will give a shoulder to cry on and sooth fears with sweet imaginary notions of God's unconditional love. He will say, Jesus has done it all, there is nothing more to do. He will assure you that this is a good thing, because in reality all your faithfulness is disgusting to God, like a menstrual cloth. He will tell you that the very best you can do is actually very disgusting to God. All we have to do is believe that Jesus died for our sins, we are told. We are told by the "lawless one" to memorize John 3:16, and verses like it. We are told that this is what it means to "know Jesus," to believe that he died for my sins. He teaches that the rest is gravy, and that you can live without gravy. The darkness settles in. We already have all we need. We are saved. Roman Catholics put Jesus in their hearts by eating the host, and we put Jesus in our hearts by going forward, and praying a prayer.

We have believed a host of lies and it is time to hear Jesus again. It is time to not rest content with old path orthodoxy. Jesus Christ and His apostles can and must be understood. The Bible is a covenantal document that is not to be ripped into preferential pieces. It is meant to be eaten whole. We need all of it because all of it has been given to us to save us. We "live by every word that proceeds from the mouth of God" (Mt. 4:4). The covenant that God has made with His people incorporates the commands and the promises into one unified saving Word. Luther and Calvin were tragically wrong to lead us in another direction. But, they recognized their own fallibility. Our Lord will be their judge.

In the meantime, I personally believe (and hope!) that, though wrong about the covenant and how it functions, these were men who lived the truth. They loved Jesus Christ and suffered much for Him. They lived and worshiped better than their doctrine. Jonathan Edwards recognized this possibility when he considered "how a wonderful and mysterious agency of God's Spirit may so influence some men's hearts, that their practice in this regard may be contrary to their own principles."[32] The best testimony to this from Luther was the expression of his distress at the end of his life:

> Luther thought the preaching of the gospel would bring about all the necessary changes, but had to complain bitterly, at the end of his life, of the dissolute manners of the students and citizens at Wittenberg, and seriously thought of leaving the city in disgust.[33]

This brings to mind Peter writing about Lot as a "righteous man, who was distressed by the filthy lives of lawless men, for that righteous man, living among them day after day, was tormented in his righteous soul by the lawless deeds he saw and heard" (2 Pet. 2:7,8). In his case, Luther was bemoaning a city who had cut its teeth on faith alone teaching. He was a man who bemoaned the practice of a people that

---

32 Edwards, *Works*, Vol. 1, 654.
33 Philip Schaff, *History of The Christian Church*, Vol. 8, Hendricksen, 1996, 484-5.

had followed consistently from the principles taught. To Luther's credit, his practice was different, as he had not lived according to his own principles.

We must do better. We must teach and preach true principles. We must teach and preach the covenant of our Lord, and in doing so, be reformers according to God's Word. The light of the Lord's Word must shine on and in the church. It will expose much sin and complacency, but we will gain life and have it abundantly. The darkness will recede where the light of God's truth is proclaimed in all its covenantal pungency. In the words of Dr. C. van der Waal, "If things go wrong in the churches, ask whether the covenant is preached and understood. If the missionary work is superficial, ask whether the covenant is taken into account. If sects and movements multiply, undoubtedly they speak of the covenant in a strange way, or ignore it deliberately."[34] We must recall the words of Isaiah for our day of great darkness,

"To the law and to the testimony!
If they do not speak according to this word,
they have no light of dawn."

---

34 C van der Waal, *The Covenantal Gospel,* 175.

18.

The Covenantal Lens

It has long been recognized that nobody interacts with his or her world as a neutral observer. We all understand our environments from the context of prior experience.[35] If the only dog I had ever met had bitten me on the leg, then the next encounter with a dog would be a guarded one. I would be predisposed to have a cautious attitude toward the dog based on prior experience. The same is true of our understanding of what we read.

When we pick up our Bibles, we are coming to it predisposed to read it and understand it in certain ways. A particular brand of atheist may believe the Bible to be a collection of human myths that seek to bring hope into an otherwise hopeless world. He may read of the resurrection of Christ, just as a believer would, but his predisposition would lead him to conclude that this is not historical but mythological. He would understand this as a reflection of human yearning to provide an answer to the great problem of death. His brand of atheism is the lens by which he understands the Bible.

A Roman Catholic reads the Bible expecting passages to reinforce and confirm the teachings of the church. For instance, when a Catholic reads that Mary was the mother of Jesus and he had brothers and sisters, the church teaching on the "perpetual virginity" of Mary leads the Catholic to conclude that these brothers and sisters must not be *literally* brothers and sisters, but only close relations who are affectionately referred to as brothers and sisters. So we can see how the teachings of the church become the lens with which a Catholic understands the Scriptures.

The truth is, none of us reads the Scriptures without putting on

---

35 See John Frame's discussion in *The Doctrine of the Knowledge of God,* P&R, 1987, 126.

our particular lens, which has been fashioned by prior experience and prior knowledge. Our predispositions inform the way we understand the Bible. We need to clear the air of any naive ideas that anyone can open their Bibles with absolute objectivity. Not only is this not possible, it is not even preferable. As human beings, we are necessarily conditioned to understand present encounters by the information we have received in the past.

In order to make the point I will further develop my dog illustration used above. After meeting the first dog that resulted in my being bitten, what is needed in order to correct my fear of every dog I encounter, is not to erase my thoughts of prior experiences with dogs in order that I would achieve absolute objectivity. In reality, this would not be possible. Even if I had never seen a dog before, I would still be predisposed toward this hairy four legged creature by my experience of similar animals in the past.

We are always gathering information from prior experience in order to make the best possible evaluation of new experiences. What I would need is not detached objectivity, but more information about dogs. I would need more experiences with various kinds of dogs in all kinds of situations, then I would be better at making a correct evaluation of potential danger. The lens through which I see and understand dogs becomes sharpened and more precise.

When we come to the Bible, it will not work to say we must get rid of all predispositions in order to properly understand it. We cannot tell the Catholic that they must try to read the Bible without their lens of traditional church teaching and read it objectively. Rather, what we must suggest, is that traditional church teachings that have evolved though the centuries may not be the best lens to use in seeking to understand documents written centuries before those doctrines ever existed. If the doctrine of the perpetual virginity of Mary came into being hundreds of years after Mark wrote his Gospel, then it is not at all likely that Mark had that doctrine in mind as he wrote about Mary and Jesus Christ in his Gospel.

The same is true for modern evangelicalism. It is well documented that modern evangelicals read their Bibles through the lens of the justification by faith alone doctrine.[36] People are predisposed to

---

36 In the book, Justification by Faith Alone, Dr. Joel Beeke makes the point that the faith alone doctrine "was the key that unlocked the Bible for Luther." All the contributors to this book reflect this mindset as they seek to defend what they

see this doctrine in the Scriptures because they open their Bibles with their lenses in place, ready to see this teaching on every page.

There is a difference here between the evangelical and the Catholic. It will not be sufficient to suggest to the evangelical that it may not be best to interpret the Scriptures by a doctrine that Martin Luther discovered in the 16th Century, because the evangelical does not claim to stand on traditional church teaching, but on Scripture alone. So the evangelical believes that the lens he wears is biblically derived. For them, Martin Luther's eyes were opened to the true meaning of the Bible.

On this point, the evangelical position is far superior to the Catholic. The evangelical recognizes that God has manifested His will in a special way through the Scriptures, and it is only through the Bible that we are able to discern the wisdom the truthfulness of our traditions. The Catholic, in reality, holds church tradition in a higher place than Scripture, because the historical church teaching becomes the lens by which the Scriptures are understood. This opens the way for the Bible to be interpreted with the intention of harmonizing it with tradition, or to put it more negatively, to wrest it from the intended meaning of the original authors and make it an advocate of what the church has come to believe. Because the church teaches the perpetual virginity of Mary, Jesus' "brothers and sisters" could not be Mary's children, even though there is nothing in the biblical context that would suggest otherwise. This particular lens serves to distort rather than clarify original intent. In contrast, the evangelical seeks to fashion his lens from the proper source which is the Scriptures understood in their historical context.

Again, we can employ our dog illustration in order to show why this is most appropriate. To put it simply, if you want to understand dogs you don't study chipmunks. The lens of predisposed understanding is fashioned from the study of what you want to understand. Experiencing many different kinds of dogs in various contexts serves to sharpen my lens when encountering a dog I have never met before. I am predisposed by past encounters in order to accurately understand new ones. When I approach a dog who is wagging his tail with his tongue hanging out and head close to the ground, I know that we have a friendly dog because one that behaves

---

understand to be traditional reformed orthodoxy. See Justification by Faith Alone: Affirming the Doctrine by which the Church Stands or Falls, Soli Deo Gloria, 2003.

like that has never bitten me.

Likewise, the Scriptures provide the lens with which we are to understand the Scriptures. This is the understanding that informed John Calvin's writing of his *Institutes of the Christian Religion.* The Institutes are the fruit of Calvin's understanding of biblical teaching. His book was to be read as a lens, or an interpretational guide, by which the average Christian was to understand the Scriptures.[37] However, he also taught that the Scriptures were to evaluate his *Institutes.*[38] For Calvin, the Bible was the tool that would sharpen his lens (the *Institutes*) in order to better understand the Scriptures. This is also the logic of the evangelical Scotch Confession of 1560. The Confession is understood to be a sum of biblical teaching and the average Christian is to read the Scriptures through the lens of the Confession. However, the writers of the Confession wisely incorporated the possibility of being corrected by the Scriptures themselves as they included this provision:

> We protest that if anyone will note in this our Confession any article or sentence repugnant to God's Holy Word, that it would please him of his gentleness and for Christian charity's sake, to admonish us of the same in writing; and we, upon our honor and fidelity, by God's grace, do promise him satisfaction from the mouth of God (that is, from the Holy Scriptures), or else reformation of that which he shall prove amiss.[39]

As in all of life, and because we are human and not divine, we will always be growing in our understanding. Because we believe the Scriptures to be the baseline of our understanding, we must always be open to the possibility of our predispositions or lenses undergoing

---

37 Calvin exhorts people to read his book by writing, "I exhort all those who have reverence for the Lord's Word, to read it, and to impress it diligently upon their memory if they wish to have, first, a sum of Christian doctrine, and, secondly, a way to benefit greatly from reading the Old as well as the New Testament." *Institutes,* Vol. 1, pg. 8. Also, "For I believe I have embraced the sum of religion in its parts, and have arranged it in such an order, that if anyone rightly grasps it, it will not difficult for him to determine what he ought especially to seek in Scripture, and to what end he ought to relate its contents" (4).

38 Calvin closes his note to the reader of the *Institutes* by writing, "Above all, I must urge him to have recourse to the Scripture in order to weigh the testimonies that I have adduced from it" (8).

39 Philip Schaff, *The History of the Creeds,* Baker, 1998, 683.

necessary correction and adjustment. In this sense we are always being reformed according to the light God has provided in His Word.

In this book, we operate with the same commitment to the foundational authority of the Scriptures. However, while Luther considered justification by faith alone to be his *biblically derived* lens, and Calvin considered the Institutes to be his *biblically derived* lens for the people, we advocate that the covenant God has made with His people to be the only reliable lens for understanding the Scriptures. Everything can and should be understood as an aspect within the covenant. The reason for this is straight-forward. If the Old and New Testament are documents of the covenant, then it stands to reason that the covenant will provide a reliable interpretational framework for understanding the information contained therein. The biblical concept of justification needs to be understood in terms of how that term functions *within* the covenant. The meaning of the Lords' Supper needs to be understood, not in terms of the platonic philosophical concepts of substance and accidence, but in terms of how the Passover meal functioned *within* the covenant. The covenant is the overarching framework.

Since the Bible is a collection of documents written within a covenantal relationship with God, it stands to reason that the covenant needs to be understood in order to understand the documents within it. Of course, it is from the Scriptures that the covenant is understood as God's authoritative communication to the world, and conversely, it is from that biblical understanding (shall we say, *informed* predisposition) that the Scriptures are understood. Scripture (the biblical covenant) interprets Scripture (all the biblical documents) and conversely, Scripture (all the biblical documents) correct and adjust our understanding of Scripture (the biblical covenant).

As I have illustrated, the best way to understand dogs is to study dogs. The study of other animals may provide helpful supplemental information, but encounters with dogs provides the understanding that will keep me safe. Likewise, while the study of other writings may offer helpful information (i.e. philosophy, church history, Hittite treaties, Josephus, 2 Maccabees), there is nothing like sitting down with God's correspondence to understand God. There is nothing like understanding the covenant God has made with man in history in order to understand what Paul meant by "the righteousness of God" in his letter to the church in Rome.

As should be evident by now, this chapter is a call for Roman Catholics and Protestants to begin reading their Bibles differently, not through the lens of church tradition, or through a particular doctrine like justification by faith alone, nor through Calvin's Institutes. God Himself has provided the interpretational framework by which we are to understand His inspired writings. My hope is that by the time the reader has reached this point in the book and has seen how God's covenant does not change in its structure and logic from Adam to Jesus, and that the documents themselves reflect this consistent logic, that this proposal would not seem radical and outlandish, but obvious. Yes, it makes sense that to understand individual dogs, you must have experience with dogs. In order to understand how we are justified within the covenant, we must understand how that covenant functions. What this amounts to, is a call away from traditions of all kinds, which function as unquestioned authorities by which the Scriptures are distorted. It is a call to be truly reformed according to the Word of God.

Someone at this point may object, "Wait a minute, we evangelicals stand on Scripture alone just as you have said, so how can you be calling us away from tradition?" This book is an attempt to show how evangelicals are wrong to teach and believe in justification by faith alone. Far too many *assume* this doctrine to be correct and are unwilling to question it.[40] Far too many resort to biblically incoherent arguments, or authoritative scare tactics and theological bullying, in order to defend what they think is necessary for the church to be faithful to God.[41]

This doctrine has become the *assumed* guardian of evangelical orthodoxy. At the level of interpretation, it now functions as the unquestioned lens that "unlocks the Bible" in the same way that tradition does for the Catholic. This is true because of the evangelical

---

40 I have had many interactions where faith alone was considered by pastors to be a "non-negotiable" of their creed. In other words, they would not even begin to entertain that they might be wrong. I have been rejected from evangelical communion on the basis of the statement "that is not what we have always believed" and by that fact that I am out of line with their confession. When attempting to discuss this crucial doctrine with my deacons in a church I was confronted with a stack of Protestant creeds as evidence for the fact that I was wrong. These encounters serve to illustrate the problem.

41 See my paper "Smoke and Mirrors: Refuting Fallacious Arguments for Justification by Faith Alone." This is a response to the book *Justification by Faith Alone,* with contributions from John MacArthur, R.C. Sproul and John Gerstner among others. This can be found on www.covenantofchrist.org.

refuses to allow Scripture to modify doctrine in the same way that the Catholic refuses Scripture to modify tradition. You can't have two masters. The church will be a slave to God in submission to His will as revealed in the Scriptures, or the church will enslave the Scriptures to her own ideas and values. The way of humility is to *always* be willing to be instructed by the Word of God. This is the true evangelical way as reflected in those who came before us. The way of stiff-necked pride is to stand your ground and shut your ears to new encounters with the Word of God that challenges "what we have always believed." This is the way of idolatry and death.

The way of life is the way of humility. The way of humility wants to hear God and is willing to change and repent of any article of doctrine that is shown to be out of step with His Word. We must remember, God is our judge, not the Pope, nor Luther or Calvin. God's standard will not be the Second Vatican Council, or the Westminster Standards. It will be the covenant He has made with us. We will be judged according to the covenant of God.

Appendix:

Storming the Strong Towers of Faith Alone

In the main body of this book I have not dealt with central passages that have been advanced in support of the "justification by faith alone" doctrine. My intent in writing this book has been to demonstrate the uniform way in which the covenant has functioned from Adam through the New Covenant in Christ, the second Adam. I have tried to avoid the significant detours that would be required to address important passages marshaled in defense of the faith alone teaching. This appendix has been dedicated to that crucial task. I have selected three Pauline texts that are broadly considered to be the strong towers of faith alone teaching by its own adherents.

First, it must be acknowledged that taking a biblical position on any biblical doctrine results in the need to explain passages that appear to contradict the position taken if the position being put forward is to be shown to be biblically coherent. Faith alone adherents have to explain how James doesn't mean what he says when he asserts that "a man is justified by works and not by faith alone." The need to explain what James really meant is to say that James, on the surface, seems to assert works as a necessary means of acceptance before God. Faith alone teachers don't believe he really means this, and the responsibility lies with them to present a biblical rationale of why this is so. They must not be rejected out of hand. They deserve a fair hearing, because it is true that in our communication with each other, through normal use of language, we don't always mean what we seem to say on the surface. For example, Paul can write in Romans 5:13, "before the law was given, sin was in the world. But sin is not taken into account when there is no law." Does Paul mean what he seems to be saying? Is Paul teaching a type of universalism in which men who never hear the word of God are not responsible for their sin? On the surface, this appears to be the case. But a closer look at the immediate context and other passages concerning the accountability of man, before the giving of the law, reveals otherwise. A closer look reveals Paul to be speaking about being accountable for "transgression" of specific commands within a covenant verses a general guilt shared by all and penalized by death (Rom.5:14). To explain Paul here is not equivocating the truth, but rather its opposite. It is a pursuit of a right understanding of a particular text from Scripture as a whole. We understand what Paul meant in light of contextual considerations and other passages which address the same issue under consideration. Faith alone teachers must explain James 2:20-24, Romans 2:5-16 and Matthew 6:14,15 which would appear, on the surface, to teach justification by works and not by faith alone. I must explain passages like Galatians 3:10-12, Romans 4:1-6 and Romans 10:1-13 which would appear, on the surface, to teach justification by faith alone. If the view of the covenant that I espouse is to be accepted, then these passages must be explained. And they must be explained because they appear to teach that faith alone saves a person. My intention is to demonstrate that they don't mean what they appear to say.

I hope to have shown by this brief discussion that explanations should not be dismissed out of hand, but only rejected when shown to be a biblically incoherent explanation. For as I have said before, we all have some explaining to do.

Strong Tower # 1

All who rely on works of the law are under a curse, for it is written: "Cursed is everyone who does not continue to do everything written in the Book of the Law." Clearly no one is justified before God by the law, because, "The righteous will live by faith." The law is not based on faith; on the contrary, "The man who does these things will live by them." Christ redeemed us from the curse of the law by becoming a curse for us, for it is written, "Cursed is everyone who is hung on a tree." (Galatians 3:10-13)

It is easy to see why this passage has been a strong tower of faith alone teaching. Here Paul appears to make a sharp distinction between faith and the keeping of the law. He appears to hold up faith as the only way to be justified in contrast to keeping the law which requires the doing of it. He seems to uphold Habakkuk's "The righteous will live by faith" as the faith-way of justification and rejects Moses' "The man who does these things will live by them" as a futile law-way to be justified. This seems to be supported by Paul's further claim that "the law is not based on faith." Or, in other words, the law-way of being justified is not based on faith but rather on doing the works of it. Martin Luther states,

> Paul therefore reasoneth here, out of plain testimony of the prophet, that there is none which obtaineth justification and life before God, but the believing man, who obtaineth righteousness and everlasting life without the law, and without charity, by faith alone. The reason is, because the law is not of faith, or anything belonging to faith, for it believeth not: neither are works of the law faith, nor yet of faith: therefore faith is a thing much differing from the law. For the promise is not apprehended by working, but by believing. Yea, there is a great difference between the promise and the law, and consequently between faith and works, as there is between heaven and earth. It is impossible therefore that faith should be of the law. For faith only resteth in the promise, it only apprehended and knoweth God, and standeth only in receiving good things from God. Contrariwise the law and works consist in exacting, in doing, and giving unto God.

Clearly for Luther Galatians 3:10-13 is Paul's objective and systematic teaching on how faith and obedience relate covenantally. They stand "contrariwise" or at odds with each other. Moreover, the reason a person who tries to be justified by the law is under a curse is that it cannot be kept in the way the law itself requires it to be kept. John Calvin writes,

> Let us now see if there is any man living who satisfies the law. It is certain that none has been or ever can be found. Every individual is here condemned...Whoever has come short in any part of the law is cursed. All are held chargeable of this guilt.

Therefore all are cursed.[42]

However, a closer look at faith and the law raises some important questions concerning the Calvin's interpretation of Paul's intent in this passage. First, James claims that Abraham obtained the promise not from faith alone but from working. "Was not our ancestor Abraham justified by works when he offered his son Isaac on the altar" (Jas.2:21)? This is consistent with what is stated in Genesis 22:17,18, "Your descendants will take possession of the cities of their enemies, and through your offspring all nations on earth will be blessed, because you have obeyed me." Abraham's obedience to the command of God was the basis or ground of his apprehending the promise. James is simply restating what was reported in Genesis 22. This seems to contradict Paul's assertion that "the promise is not apprehended by working, but by believing." This was Martin Luther's own view of James, that James contradicted Paul.

Secondly, the law itself, according to Jesus Christ, commanded faith as of first importance. We read this in Matthew 23:23, "Woe to you, teachers of the law and Pharisees, you hypocrites! You give a tenth of your spices— mint, dill and cummin. But you have neglected the more important matters of the law— justice, mercy and faith. You should have practiced the latter without neglecting the former." Here Jesus places faith as one of the more important matters of the law. And this is precisely what we see there. The law itself contained remembrances of God's power in order to inspire faith in the Lord. Israel was to remember in order that they might believe or have faith. This is what Israel was so roundly criticized for. They were seen as rebels because of their failure to believe God.

"Then they despised the pleasant land; they did not *believe* his promise. They grumbled in their tents and did not obey the Lord." (Psalm 106:24, 25)

"The waters covered their adversaries; not one of them survived. Then they believed his promises and sang his praise. But they soon forgot what he had done and did not wait for his counsel." (Psalm 106:12, 13)

Here we see the connection between remembering and

---

42 Calvin, Galatians Commentary p.53

believing. To forget, for the Psalmist, is to no longer believe. The law commands festivals like the Passover in order that the people would remember and believe. It was believing that the ancients were commended for in Hebrews 11. Moses, the giver of the law, was a man of faith. In Hebrews 11 we learn that Moses kept the law by faith in order to receive the promise of God's salvation from Egyptian slavery. "By faith he left Egypt, not fearing the king's anger; he persevered because he saw him who is invisible. By faith he kept the Passover and the sprinkling of blood, so that the destroyer of the firstborn would not touch the firstborn of Israel" (Heb.11:28).

Once again, we can understand how Jesus can say that a more important matter of the law is faith, because it is by faith that the law is kept. "By faith Moses kept the Passover." From this it follows that every Passover, Sabbath, New Moon festival and whatever else was commanded was to be kept by faith. So it seems quite clear that the basis of keeping the law is, in fact, faith. This then raises an important question. If this is true, what can Paul mean when he says, "The law is not based on faith, on the contrary, 'The man who does these things will live by them'"(Gal.3:12)?

If we understand that faith was commanded in the law and indeed was kept by faith, we are now prepared to understand what Paul meant when he said that "the law is not based on faith." First, we need to recognize that Paul was not making an abstract theological statement. We need to take stock of the fact that Paul was engaging in verbal warfare against opponents of the message he preached. In polemical rhetoric it is characteristic to speak in narrow and pointed ways in order to make a particular point emphatic. For example, Ronald Reagan spoke rhetorically when he called the Soviet Union an "evil empire." By making this statement he was not making a scientific and objective moral evaluation of every citizen of the former Soviet Union. He did not mean to say that every individual within the Soviet empire was morally evil. What he meant was that the communistic world-view and political agenda that this world-view spawned had evil effects for mankind. This was powerfully communicated by the phrase "evil empire." The many critics of Reagan jumped on this phrase as being simple-minded and backward. They argued that there were many well-intentioned people in Russia and that this kind of language painted a whole nation unfairly with a broad brush. However, the critics, either intentionally or not, failed to recognize the purpose behind Reagan's use of such language. A husband or wife may employ verbal rhetoric in an argument at home. A wife who is frustrated may exclaim, "You never help me around the house!" Once again, this is not meant to be a scientific evaluation of his behavior. He may respond by saying, "What do you mean? I washed the dishes twice last month!" She would respond, "That is not what I mean. I know you help sometimes, but we are both busy with our jobs and I am the one who is expected to get things done around here." So she used a powerful statement in order to make a point. The word "never" does not mean literally and objectively, never. It means there is a severe problem with the current arrangement. This is how language is customarily used.

Paul's wrestling with the law-keeping Judaizers led him to employ this kind of polemical rhetoric repeatedly. We read this in 1 Timothy 1:9,10, "We also know that the law is made not for the righteous but for lawbreakers and rebels, the ungodly and sinful, the unholy and irreligious; for those who kill their fathers or mothers, for murderers, for adulterers and perverts, for slave traders and liars and perjurers..."

According to Paul here, the law is instituted for "perverts" and not for the righteous. How do we square this with the fact that David and many others rejoiced that the law was wisdom from God for them, and that these men and women were considered by God to be righteous according to that law? Is Paul saying that David, Hezekiah, Josiah and Elizabeth were in reality "perverts" and parent killers? Of course not. Paul is making a powerful rhetorical statement. The context reveals that he is saying that those who proclaim the need for law-keeping are in reality acting "contrary to sound doctrine," which is the gospel of Christ (1 Tim.1:10,11). This is a powerful way of saying that these people are in reality morally bankrupt in the eyes of God. The law is now for morally bankrupt people, because it is the immoral who turn away from the gospel in order to embrace the law. This graphically proclaims how reprehensible it is to desire to live "under the law" now that Christ has come.

Paul uses polemical rhetoric in Colossians 2:8, where he describes teachings that promote law-keeping as "hollow and deceptive philosophy, which depends on human tradition and the basic principles of this world..." Similarly, in Galatians 4:8,9, he describes the law as "weak and miserable principles" that enslaved them as if they were gods to them. This is incredible! God's revealed word is a "principle of this world" that even promotes idolatry? Wasn't it the law that condemned idolatry over and over again? How could the law given from God Himself, and everywhere recognized as righteous, holy and good be "miserable principles"? These were precisely the questions that he was provoking others to ask. What Paul is condemning here is not the law objectively considered. The law, Paul reports in Romans 7:12 is "holy, righteous and good." This is his objective evaluation of the law. The law consists of righteous and holy decrees, which are not from this sinful world, but from a holy and good God. But how could he call them "weak and miserable principles"? We read what Paul wrote, but we must know what Paul meant when he wrote these words. We know from Romans 8:3 what Paul meant. He did not mean that they were, in themselves, weak. He meant that "the law was powerless...in that it was weakened by the sinful nature" (Rom.8:3). What is miserable and weak are human beings under the law, because they are enslaved by the sinful nature. Moreover, it is not through the law that God ultimately has ordained to set men free from the guilt and power of sin, but in Christ. The law was a mere pointer or shadow of the reality (Col.2:17). God's power through the Holy Spirit is not manifested now through the law but through Christ. The law is now a weak and miserable principle because God's power is no longer to be found there. This is how Paul can consider these people to be enslaved by "gods" of the law. Works of the law have themselves become as gods to them, enslaving them, because they have to turn away from the one true God who is Jesus Christ in order to embrace them. Furthermore, this is how Paul can refer to the law as "hollow philosophies" and the "teachings based on human tradition." Christ was always the true substance of the law, so when you turn from Jesus Christ in order to embrace the law, you are turning the law into a "human teaching," a "hollow philosophy." It has been emptied of its God-centered substance and a shell of a weak and miserable man-made religion is left behind.

In all of this powerful rhetoric Paul is not making objective, scientific, timeless statements about the law as a phenomenon of God's revelation. The words inscribed by God's finger on Moses' stone tablets were not "miserable principles." Rather, they were to be the very opposite for God's people—their great delight and joy as expressions of God's will for His people (see Psalm 119). Neither were they ever considered to be "hollow philosophies." Such a sentiment would get you justly stoned for blasphemy under the direction of that same law.

When Paul wrote Galatians, he was addressing an historical situation of false teachers who were misusing the law in specific ways. Paul's expressions reflect, not the law itself objectively considered, but a particular strand of the law's misuse. The tragedy here is that Luther did not seem to appreciate this. For him, the law was, as God's revelation through Moses, a "miserable principle." For Luther it was not the misuse of it that made it so, but its proper use as the condemner of sin.

Not surprisingly, we read the same kind of rhetorical language used in 1 Timothy and Colossians in the passage under consideration in Galatians 3, because Paul is dealing with the same opponents in all three letters. "The law is not based on faith" means the law as it is being promoted by the false teachers he is addressing. Paul's point, is not that the law had nothing to do with faith to uphold it, but that faith has a transcendent life of its own which is based on the promise and not based on the law of Moses. Faith believes the promise, this is the indispensable core of God's interaction with men, which (and this is the important point for Paul) transcends the law. God speaks and we must believe. On the occasion of hearing the promise, faith is the obedience required (Gen.15:1-6). The first and overarching necessity, in order for obedience to be possible, was faith in the promise. The law requires "the doing of it," this is from Moses and true enough, but the promise requires faith. The false teachers are failing to believe this word of promise by continuing to embrace works of the law. The promise of the gospel is that all the promises of the Old Covenant "find their 'yes' in Jesus Christ" and only in Jesus Christ. Since it is found exclusively by faith in Jesus, then it is not in keeping the law (2 Cor.1:20). The false teachers are not believing that promise, by embracing "works of the law" as necessary for justification. This teaching requires Paul to make this antithetical statement, "not doing, but believing." To live by the law is to do it, but to live by the promise is to believe it. The promise believed was how Abraham's relationship with the Lord was initiated. Abraham was justified from the moment he believed the promise. Abraham was justified years prior and without the giving of the Mosaic law. In this sense, Abraham was justified apart from the doing of the law and by faith. What Paul meant is that the law is not permanently binding, and Abraham is an ideal example in retrospect, because Abraham was the esteemed father of the Jews—who was justified apart from law—just as the Gentiles and Jews are now. But the promise continues and is permanently offered in the gospel of Jesus Christ and faith in that promise remains the saving response to that promise.

Third, when Paul says those "of the works of the law" can't be justified because, "cursed is everyone who does not continue to do everything written in the Book of the Law," he is not making a statement about the impossibility of doing all of it. He can't mean this because the Scriptures reveal that the law was able to be kept. This reality contradicts Calvin and Luther's belief that Galatians 3:10 contains a suppressed premise that the law could not be kept—that it was and is impossible to keep all of it. So, they would understand it this way:

> All who rely on works of the law are under a curse, *(suppressed premise: for no one can keep the law)* and it is written, "Cursed is everyone who does not continue to do everything written in the Book of the Law."

The understanding above cannot be true because of the simple fact that in many places the laws, regulations and decrees were reported to be have been done successfully. The following three examples make this clear:

"As for you, if you walk before me as your father David did, and do all I command, and observe my decrees and laws, I will establish your royal throne" (2 Chronicles 7:17).

"Neither before nor after Josiah was there a king like him who turned to the Lord as he did—with all his heart and with all his soul and with all his strength, in accordance with all the Law of Moses" (2 Kings 23:25).

"Both of them were upright in the sight of God, observing all the Lord's commandments and regulations blamelessly" (Luke 1:6).

These clear statements of Scripture establish Calvin's suppressed premise that the law could not be kept as biblically untenable. So we must revisit Paul's statement and inquire again as to why Paul would insist on a curse for those who "rely on works of the law?" I believe that a more biblical and historically sensitive understanding of this statement understands Paul to be rejecting "those who rely on works of the law" or more literally, those who are "of the works of the law" as people who were asserting specific statements about what people must do in order to be saved. This historical group of people is no mystery to us, and neither is what they were teaching. From Acts 15, Galatians and Romans 4, it is abundantly clear that Paul is rejecting teachers who were saying, not only must you believe in Jesus, but you also must believe in Moses. But these teachers were not in the first order asserting all of Moses, they were emphasizing what they considered certain non-negotiables of the Mosaic law. This why they were called "the circumcision group" (Gal.2:12; Tit 1:10). Circumcision was the primary push of these teachers as Acts 15 and Paul's statements make clear. This is not to say that Paul did not discern the slippery slope of this teaching, and indeed, there were those sliding down it, and now observing special days, dietary restrictions, etc. (Gal.4:9). But the central thrust of these teachers consisted in the continuing necessity of non-negotiable Mosaic commands. The tip of this Mosaic law iceberg was the teaching of the necessity of circumcision. This makes good Old Covenant sense, because circumcision was the entry rite into the Old Covenant people of God. For them, this was the first and primary step of becoming truly saved and accepted by God. Paul is throwing the law's own teachings back at these men who teach certain non-negotiables of the law as needing to be done. If you are under the law, according to its own witness, you are under all of it and not just self- chosen portions. These men who asserted the law, were not speaking according to the law's own expectations and requirements for covenantal fidelity. Paul wrote in Galatians 5:3, "Again, I declare to every man who lets himself be circumcised that he is obligated to obey the whole law." Paul has to say this because this is something the false teachers were not saying, even though once sold on circumcision, many were coming to this logical conclusion. The law, by definition, was something to be swallowed whole. The law of Moses begins and ends with this assertion, and this is spoken over and over again throughout the law.

"Hear now, O Israel, the decrees and laws I am about to teach you. Follow them so that you may live and may go in and take possession of the land that the Lord, the God of your fathers, is giving you. Do not add to what I command you and do not subtract from it, but keep the commands of the Lord your God that I give you." (Deut. 4:1, 2)

"'Cursed is the man who does not uphold *the words of this law by carrying them out.*' Then all the people shall say, 'Amen!'" (Deut. 27:26)

These men were teaching certain "works of the law" as necessary, so Paul quotes Deuteronomy 27:26 in order to show how their teaching leads to being under the law's curse. They teach people to do certain things in the law, while the law itself commands you to do all things or be cursed, therefore to follow the "works of the law" teachers is to be cursed according the law's own expectation. Paul states, "Not even those who are circumcised obey the law, yet they want you to be circumcised that they may boast about your flesh" (Gal.6:13). This makes much better sense of this passage, because it is a biblical fact, as we have seen, that the law could be and was kept by faithful Israelites.

Secondly, to be "under the law" was to be under the law as a curse in two possible senses. First, the law was given as a national charter. The law of Moses was a law for the nation of Israel by definition. Therefore it was to be kept by the nation. It was the nation as a whole that would stand or fall by the law of Moses. By the time Paul wrote this letter it was an established fact that the nation as a whole had broken God's covenant and were under his curse, as we see clearly from the prophets. Once the covenant had been broken, the promised curses of Deuteronomy were poured out on the nation. What was in effect at the time of the writing of Galatians was the promised curses under the covenant of the Mosaic law. To be under the law was to be under a national curse of famine, plague, and foreign oppression.

However, this is not to say that the Lord had no regard for righteous individuals within the nation of Israel. There was always a faithful remnant within the nation, maintaining covenant loyalty to the one true God. This finds classic expression in Elijah who bemoaned the corporate infidelity of Israel under Ahab's ungodly and idolatrous leadership. Elijah thought he was the only individual to remain faithful, but the Lord informed him that there were seven thousand other individuals within unfaithful Israel who has remained faithful to the covenant and had not bowed the knee to Baal (Romans 11:3,4; 1 Kings 19:10). Also, we see God turning his back on the nation with Manasseh's infidelity, yet after His back was turned, it could be said about Josiah, a king to come later, "Neither before nor after Josiah was there a king like him who turned to the Lord as he did—with all his heart and with all his soul and with all his strength, in accordance with the law of Moses" (2 Kings 23:25). Josiah, as an individual, was faithful in the midst of a continuously unfaithful nation. So we can say that even though the nation was under a curse, there were covenant-keeping individuals who nevertheless had God's favor. It is not as though these faithful ones were kept from the suffering produced by the curse over the nation. They as well would killed by invading armies, enslaved in Babylon, and experience the hunger and oppression this national curse produced. God knew them as faithful ones in the midst of an unfaithful nation and their hope would transcend their present suffering. Nehemiah, a faithful man who worked tirelessly for the holiness of unfaithful Israel reflects this hope, "Remember me for this also, O my God, and show mercy to me according to your great love" (Neh.13:22).

So it is biblically possible to speak of two senses in which a person could experience the curse of the law. To be an Israelite was to be under the national curse. But it is also true a person could be under God's mercy, or have his favor, like Elijah, Nehemiah, Josiah, Zechariah, Elizabeth, and Jesus Himself, who was born "under law," while at the same time living under a national curse. From this we can see that the worst of all situations was to be under God's curse in total and to have no national or personal hope of God's favor. To be an unfaithful individual was to not only experience the national curse, but also God's curse on you as an individual without a hope that transcends the present circumstances. It is to not only have God as your national enemy, but to have God as your personal enemy as well. Keeping part of the law, as the Judaizers had been teaching, places you not just under the national curse of Israel, but also under God's personal curse, because, as we have already seen, the law as a whole must be kept. Here, it is important to note, that Paul seeks to undermine the false teachers according to their own false premise of the necessity of law-keeping post-Christ. He is not to be understood as endorsing the proper keeping of the law. He is demonstrating that these men are tragically wrong-headed even according to law-keeping standards, which they claim to uphold.

Paul also asserts that no one is justified by the law but by Christ. Once again, it is crucial to understand this as a polemical statement. He is responding to those who assert law-keeping after Jesus Christ, the fulfillment of the law of Moses, has come. Paul would have had no problem asserting law-keeping as God's requirement pre-Christ. However, the law finds its true meaning and substance in Christ. Therefore, to be justified under the law, as many were, is in reality to be justified by Christ, since He is the true meaning of the law. So what Paul meant is that ultimately no one is justified by the law. Once Christ comes, the law loses its significance, since its significance was as a reflection of Christ. He is not saying that the law was never kept, or could not be kept, or that the doing of it was somehow wrongheaded (see Luke 1:6). Still less is he saying that faith had nothing to do with law-keeping (see Hebrews 11:28). Neither is he saying that there was nothing Abraham had to do in order to be justified (see James 2:20-24). His point in Galatians is polemically specific and has to with "works of the law" post-Christ and not obedience generally considered. To those who assert law keeping post-Christ, no one is justified that way now, because in reality, no one ultimately and in light of the revelation of Jesus Christ, was ever justified in that way. This is how he can talk about law-keeping as doing and not believing (Galatians 3:11,12). This is how Paul can pit Moses against Habakkuk.

As an objective reality, Habakkuk, the prophet of faith, was not opposed to Moses, the teacher of the law. If Habakkuk had been asked if law-keeping was required in order to accepted by the Lord, he would have responded with a resounding "Yes!" In fact, it is the lack of law-keeping in Israel that caused him such personal grief (Hab.1:4). If Moses had been asked if the Israelites needed to have faith in order to be accepted by their covenant Lord, he would have said unequivocally "Yes!" Moses, was a model of Old Covenant faith (Heb.11:28). Paul can and does pit Moses' required "doing" against Habakkuk's required "faith," because of the teachings of the post-Christ law-keepers. To have Moses now that Christ has come, is by necessity, to dispense with faith in the promise. Paul is responding to the error of asserting Moses, because to assert Moses is to deny faith in the promise. They claim Moses as still binding, but to do so is to reject Habakkuk. This is why Paul asserts Habakkuk over Moses. What Habakkuk proclaimed remains binding and true in Christ, while what Moses proclaimed by way of commandments has been fulfilled in Christ (Matt.5:17). The righteous still live by faith, but the law has become obsolete (Heb.8:13).

This I believe pulls it all together. Paul's anti-law and pro-faith-in-the-promise statements are specifically designed to reject the false teaching confronting the church. These men want to retain certain cherished practices of the law as necessary for acceptance. Paul rejects the doing of the law and upholds faith in the promise in the face of this threat. To retain the law is to reject faith-in-the promise, since Jesus Christ is the fulfillment of the law and object of the promise. He is not making expansive objective statements about how faith and obedience relate to one another covenantally. He is not giving an objective theological treatise on the nature of the law as God's revelation to mankind. To understand him in this way is to miss the point of Galatians as a response to an historical error. Reformed theology has missed his point so its proponents speak as if God saves, at least theoretically, in two ways, either by law or by faith. Paul's radical antithesis, which was designed to reject a specific historical teaching, has become Reformed theology's objective and timeless way of looking at commands and faith in general. They have understood Galatians 3:10-12 to be Paul's understanding of how the "diverse" covenants work. According to them, there is a covenant of works (required doings) and covenant of grace (faith in the promise). It is easy to see how they come to this conclusion if Paul's polemic against a specific historical error is not understood.

Paul's follow-up example from 3:15-18 confirms our interpretation. This is meant to explain what preceded in 3:10-14. Paul in this section describes the temporary nature of the law. He does this by describing how God's covenant with Abraham was not annulled by the covenant of the Mosaic law, which comes later. The promise continues as well as the necessity of faith in that promise. The law, which is in the fore of the false teacher's thinking, does not supersede the covenant made with Abraham, in fact, he describes the law as being added as a temporary measure. He states, "What then was the purpose of the law? It was added because of transgressions until the Seed to whom the promise referred had come." So the law was "added" after Abraham and was to be binding "until" Christ. He concludes in 3:25, "Now that faith has come, we are no longer under the supervision of the law." His overall thrust is two things, the temporary and the overall negative role of the law. The law was temporary, and its purpose was to restrain and demonstrate Israel as sinners (along with the world). But what does Paul mean by "now that faith has come?" Does he mean the response of faith to the promise of God, which had not previously existed? He can't mean that, because as Hebrews 11 demonstrates, a whole host of people in the Old Covenant had faith in the promise. The faith that has come is the same faith as "this faith" in Galatians 3:23: "Before this faith came, we were held prisoners by the law, locked up until faith should be revealed." The faith that has come, or this specific faith, is faith in Jesus Christ as the fulfillment of the law and the promise. "The law was put in charge to lead us to Christ that we might be justified by faith"(Gal.3:24). It is crucial to continue to understand that the people of God have always been justified by faith, even under the law. The law's role here is to lead us "to Christ in order that we might be justified by faith"in Christ. The revelation of Jesus Christ is what is truly new! However, we cannot take our eyes off the ball and miss Paul's main point. Notice how this serves Paul's polemic against the law-keeper teaching: The law served its purpose "until faith should be revealed" (3:23) or in other words, "the law was put in charge to lead us to Christ that we might be justified by faith. Now that faith has come, we are no longer under the supervision of the law" (3:25).

The temporary nature of the law in God's redemptive and covenantal history is Paul's main point. The purpose of his argument is to reject the false teaching currently confronting the church which seeks to maintain the validity of the Mosaic law. To use these statements as a general teaching on how faith and obedience work covenantally without regard for Paul's narrow and historical purpose is to be ripe for misuse and misunderstanding. Paul was not pitting faith against obedience, or promise against command, he was pitting New Covenant against Old Covenant, allegiance to Jesus Christ against a misguided residual allegiance to Moses.

One thing to note in addition. Paul is not interested in arguing for the validity of Christ's claims to be the Savior of Israel and the world. Paul argues from the standpoint of those who at least acknowledge Christ as Lord. This is not a matter of debate with Paul's opponents. His concern is to show how Jesus as the fulfillment of the promise effects our view of law-keeping. The false teachers believed that law-keeping along with faith in Jesus Christ was necessary to inherit the promise. Paul's strong polemic is to show how law-keeping is not only no longer necessary, but opposed to faith in Christ. So he says, not by law, or by doing the law, but by faith in Jesus. "If the inheritance depends on the law, then it no longer depends on a promise;

but God in his grace gave it (the inheritance) to Abraham through a promise." Paul is quick to note that the law objectively considered as God's revelation is not against the promise (3:21). This is easy to see, because the promise of inheritance is contained in the law itself. The promise to Abraham is repeated to his descendants, the people of Israel, through the law (Deut. 28:1-14). But once "this faith" in Christ has come, then Old Covenant law-keeping for acceptance by God has ended.

Strong Tower #2

> What then shall we say that Abraham, our forefather, discovered in this matter? If, in fact, Abraham was justified by works, he had something to boast about—but not before God. What does the Scripture say? "Abraham believed God, and it was reckoned to him as righteousness." Now when a man works, his wages are not credited to him as a gift, but as an obligation. However, to the man who does not work but trusts God who justifies the wicked, his faith is credited as righteousness. David says the same thing when he speaks of the blessedness of the man to whom God credits righteousness apart from works: "Blessed are they whose transgressions are forgiven, whose sins are covered. Blessed is the man whose sin the Lord will never count against him." (Romans 4:1-9)

From my experience, this is the most popular text in defense of faith alone. While faith alone for justification is never spoken of favorably in the Scriptures, it is believed that this passage teaches the substance of the matter. Indeed, this would appear to be the case when Paul says in verse 5, "However, to the man who does not work but trusts God who justifies the wicked, his faith is credited as righteousness." First, Paul sets working against believing when he writes, "to the man who does not work but trusts God." He appears to be saying that working and believing for justification are antithetical to each other. This understanding is further strengthened by Paul's teaching that the man of faith is the "wicked" who stands justified by his faith. This establishes the non-worker to be the one who stands justified by his faith, because he is a wicked man who has no works to credit him before God. It is understood that David is depicted by Paul as another example to illustrate the point. David speaks of the "transgressor" who has his sins covered by faith and "apart from works" (vv. 6-8). David's own life as a forgiven sinner is understood to reflect this faith alone perspective. At first glance, this seems to be a formidable text for faith alone.

However, we have to keep in mind that Paul wrote Romans 4 as an historical illustration for his teaching from Romans 2. We see this from Paul's opening verse in Romans 4, "What then (or therefore) shall we say Abraham, our forefather discovered in this matter?" Paul is now bringing in Abraham and David as historical examples to give flesh and bones to his prior teaching. He wisely calls Abraham and David, since they were two Jewish heroes, into his argument as key witnesses. So it follows that we need to know what Paul was arguing for in Romans 2-3, in order to know how Abraham and David function as illustrations. In other words, we must understand Romans 4 in the context of Paul's overall argument. The question is: What is Paul's concern that makes Abraham and David ideal witnesses?

Paul's concern for his fellow Jews is front and center in Romans 2:17, 18, 21, 23: "Now you, if you call yourself a Jew; if you rely on the law and *brag* about your relationship to God; if you know his will and approve of what is superior because you are instructed by the law...you, then, who teach others, do you not teach yourself?...You who *brag* about the law, do you dishonor God by breaking the law?"

Here we read of Paul's strong concern about Jewish boasting. They are in the very bad habit of boasting "about their relationship to God" and "about the law." What makes this particularly offensive to Paul is that while they boast about their possession of the law and their relationship to God through it, they at the same time are in the habit of breaking it. It is important to see that their boasting does not derive from obedience to the law, but rather, their boasting derives from the mere possession of it. Paul then further critiques his fellow Jews by bringing up circumcision. It is clear that this has a disproportionate value to the Jew because Paul finds it necessary to argue against its value. "Circumcision has value if you observe the law, but if you break the law, you have become as though you were not circumcised" (Rom. 2:25). Clearly they are finding their confidence before God by circumcision even while they steal and commit adultery. Paul goes on, "If those who are not circumcised keep the law's requirements, will they not be regarded as though they were circumcised? The one who is not circumcised physically and yet obeys the law will condemn you who, even though you have the written code and circumcision, are a lawbreaker." This makes Paul's concern very clear. He is arguing against a Jewish confidence in mere possession of the law. They are deceived into thinking that having the law and bearing the physical sign of circumcision is enough. Paul argues his point in even stronger terms, "A man is not a Jew if he is one only outwardly, nor is circumcision merely outward and physical. No, a man is a Jew if he is one inwardly; and circumcision is circumcision of the heart, by the Spirit, not by the written code. Such a man's praise is not from men, but from God" (Rom. 2:28,29). Notice, Paul equates the keeping of the law with circumcision of the heart by the Spirit. In other words, the man who obeys the law is the man who has the Spirit, and the man who relies on circumcision of his flesh is the one devoid of the Spirit and a lawbreaker. The man who, by the Spirit's power, keeps the law, will at the day of judgment condemn the man who has the law and fails to keep it.

Paul's point here, is not that keeping the law (i.e. good works) is what produces the boasting. Of course, this can happen. Sinful human beings can find almost anything as fodder for boasting, even faith. But here, Paul does not fault the law keeper as the boaster, because the boaster he is writing against is the law breaker. Paul's concern is not works per se, but confidence from mere possession of the law, in which the work of circumcision is the chief sign of its possession.

Paul then anticipates an objection from his Jewish audience, and this objection Paul presents as a rhetorical question to begin chapter 3. "What advantage, then, is there in being a Jew, or what value is there in circumcision?" Notice he equates "being a Jew" and circumcision specifically. He goes on to deny that there is no advantage at all—indeed, "they have been entrusted with the very words of God." But the remainder of chapter 3 is written not to uphold the Jew as being in a special place, but to demonstrate that life under the law has served to show that Jews are sinners in need of a Savior, just like the Gentiles. "What shall we conclude then? Are we any better? Not at all! We have already made the charge that Jews and Gentiles alike are all under sin" (Rom.3:9). Paul's argument then presents the universal solution to the universal problem of sin, which is Jesus Christ and the righteousness from God that comes to all through faith in him. Jew and Gentile alike are under sin, so Jew and Gentile alike need Jesus' sacrifice of atonement to be received by faith (Rom.3:21-26).

Now Paul returns again to his original concern. "Where then is boasting? It is excluded." The law as taught by the Jews who Paul criticizes, does not provide the basis for excluding boasting, but the knowledge of sin and the one solution for all people does exclude boasting in having the law. The Jews cannot put confidence in having the law, or in other words, "being a Jew" (Rom.3:1). "For we maintain that a man is justified by faith apart from works of the law. Is God the God of the Jews only? Is he not the God of the Gentiles, too? Yes, of the Gentiles too, since there is only one God, who will justify the circumcised by faith and the uncircumcised through that same faith." Notice, equal access to the one God of all is what Paul understands as excluding boasting. The Jew can place no confidence in their natural heritage, their physical connection seen through the physical and outward rite of circumcision.

Only now can we begin to understand Paul's use of Abraham and David in Romans 4:1-9. Now Paul introduces both Abraham and David as witnesses to men of their own bloodline, who put no confidence in that bloodline, and therefore in their circumcision, but who rather lived by faith in the promise and mercy of God. Literally, Paul poses the question this way, "What, therefore, shall we say Abraham, our forefather, discovered according to the flesh?" The NIV interprets the Greek word sarka as "this matter." It stands alone in translating this word in this way, the more popular and literal rendering is "flesh."[43] Once again, boasting comes into view with verse 2. "If, in fact, Abraham was justified by works, he had something to boast about —but not before God." Context must rule our understanding of what Paul means by boasting here. His concern right up to this verse has been a concern for Jewish boasting in having the law by virtue of being

---

43 It is debated whether the prepositional phrase "according to the flesh" modifies "our forefather" or modifies the verb "found." The first option would read "our forefather according to the flesh," the second option would read "what Abraham, our forefather found according to the flesh." I have preferred the second option for contextual reasons. Grammatically, both options are possible. Paul's prior concern was to argue for the lack of value for circumcision of the "flesh" as a justifying work before God. So it seems to make the most sense to read it this way. However, it is possible Paul would be emphasizing Abraham as a bloodline descendant, and being that, what did he, "our forefather according to the flesh" discover? The upshot of all this, is that either reading serves to establish my interpretation of Paul's meaning in this text.

a Jew and not a Gentile, with circumcision as the "work" serving as a sign of the possession of the law. Paul grants, that if Abraham was justified on this basis, he indeed has a boast—"but not before God." Abraham could have considered himself as special by virtue of his "flesh" before men. But Paul now shows his boasting brothers that Abraham himself did not have this understanding. "What does the Scripture say? 'Abraham believed God, and it was reckoned to him as righteousness'"(v.3). Abraham believed God's promise to him, and it was his faith and not his flesh that commended him before God.

Next Paul uses a wage earner illustration. "Now when a man works, his wages are not considered for him as a gift, but as an obligation. However, for the man who does not work but trusts God who justifies the wicked, his faith is considered as righteousness." We must keep our contextual controls in place. The boasting that has been Paul's concern has been of a specific kind, that is, boasting in having the law by virtue of bloodline, or "of the flesh." This mindset has created a situation in which Paul's fellow Jews believe they have a claim against God, that God owes them, or is obligated to them as His special people. His wage earner point is very specific. The worker has a claim against his employer for wages in which he can boast. Paul's point here is that this totally misunderstands the real situation between God and Abraham and David. "However, to the man who does not work..." in context means, to the man who does not think his flesh by circumcision obligates God, "but trusts God who justifies the ungodly, his faith is reckoned to him as righteousness." History is on Paul's side since Abraham was called from idolatry in Mesopotamia. Abraham had no confidence in his flesh, and had no possible reason for confidence in his flesh because of that fact. Abraham believed God's promise and was reckoned righteous by virtue of his faith, not his bloodline. Next comes David. "David says the same thing when he speaks of the blessedness of the man to whom God credits righteousness apart from works." Once again, we must keep our understanding of "apart from works" in tune to Paul's concern. David put no confidence in his circumcision to justify him before God. Bloodline meant nothing to him when confronted with his sin. David was the "ungodly" murderer and adulterer who needed his sins wiped away. His confidence was in the mercy of his God to be received by faith "apart from circumcision." We must remember that Paul is contending with Jews who are thieves, murderers and adulterers, yet have confidence before God because of their "flesh" (Rom.2:22-24). David was not like them.

Paul's argument from verse 9 through 11 serves to confirm this interpretation. "Is this blessedness only for the circumcised, or also for the uncircumcised? We have been saying that Abraham's faith was credited to him as righteousness. Under what circumstances was it credited? Was it after he was circumcised, or before? It was not after, but before" (vv. 9,10)! Now Paul is driving his argument home. Abraham was credited before God as righteous apart from circumcision. There was a period of time in which circumcision was not necessary for their forefather Abraham, and neither is it necessary now. However, it is true, as a faithful Israelite under the law, you needed to be circumcised in order to be justified as belonging to God. This was a command that had to be obeyed. But Paul's point here is simple and straight-forward. There was a time when justification took place before circumcision was mandated, and now is the time when justification takes place after the law, or the time of mandated circumcision. In fact, Abraham, as a man justified "apart from works of the law"(i.e. circumcision) stood as a forerunner of all those who would in the future would be justified "apart from works of the law." Paul explains, "So then, he is the father of all who believe but have not been circumcised, in order that righteousness might be reckoned to them"(v.11). So Abraham is not just the forefather of the Jew, but also the forefather of the Gentile, not through the flesh and circumcision, but through faith in the promise of God. However, the Jews have not been pushed aside. "And he is also the father of the circumcised who not only are circumcised but who also walk in the footsteps of the faith that our forefather Abraham had before he was circumcised"(v.12). God reckons the Jew as righteous as well, but on the same ground as the Gentile, by faith in Jesus Christ, therefore there is no possible ground for boasting. Both Jew and Gentile stand on equal footing, both claim Abraham as their forefather, but both can only do this through faith in Jesus Christ.

It should be clear now why this text cannot be seen as endorsing faith alone for justification. When Paul rejects works in this context, he is rejecting a particular kind of working that establishes a Jewish boast against other men and sees God as obligated to them by virtue of their flesh which indicates natural descent not moral effort. The extent of Paul's purpose in Romans 4 is to present historical examples that demonstrate the fallacy of this belief. He is not arguing against works in total.[44] He is not even arguing against the necessity of circumcision under the Old Covenant. He would readily acknowledge that both David and Abraham had to be circumcised in order to be justified before God. David could not confess his sin against God on the one hand and refuse God when He commands circumcision on the other and expect to be justified.

To understand Paul as rejecting "works" (i.e. obedience) in total because works by necessity result in boasting before God is to say that when God commands obedience for justification, He commands men to enter into a situation in which they will, by necessity, boast against God and sin.[45] So from this view, God commands men to sin, when He commands them to obey! It may be objected that God's commands only result in this hopeless situation when He commands obedience for justification, but not for sanctification. This objection is really no objection at all. It is a shallow attempt to avoid the obvious. If boasting against God is a sin, and boasting by necessity results from doing good works, then it really makes no difference. If good works by necessity

44 Tom Schreiner, in order to defend the traditional understanding which maintains that Paul means "works fundamentally" must deny these contextual indicators. He states, "This view founders (in the present context) because Paul does not even use the word nomos (law) in verses 1-8. The use of erga ("works") alone (v.v.2,6) and the verbal form ergazomeno ("to the one working," vv.4,5) demonstrate that his attack is against works fundamentally." Here Schreiner rejects that Paul means "works of the law," because the word "law" is never used in verses 1-8, even though "works" clearly means "works of the law" in the argument leading up to and following verses 1-8! He goes on, "To appeal to the discussion of circumcision in verses 9-12 in support of the notion of boundary markers are the central issue fails, because the "therefore" in verse 9 reveals a new stage in the argument." What Schreiner casually passes over is the fact the "therefore" connects what follows to what precedes by way of logical progression. The "therefore" points to a conclusion which is reached on the basis of what precedes. What precedes, namely verses 1-8, leads to the conclusion stated in verses 9-12. The fact that Schreiner has to dismiss this as a "new stage" and denies the obvious logical connection reveals the weakness of his position. See Schreiner, Romans: An Exegetical Commentary on the New Testament. Baker, 1998, 218.

45 John Murray demonstrates this logic in his commentary. He writes, "It (Paul's argument) is to the effect of the following syllogism. (1) If a man is justified by works he has a ground for glorying. (2) Abraham was justified by works. (3) Therefore Abraham had ground for glorying. Paul emphatically challenges and denies the conclusion...by showing the minor premise to not be true. He proves that Abraham was not justified by works and, by proving this, he refutes the conclusion."(p.130) See Murray, The Epistle to the Romans, Eerdmanns 1959, 130.

134

result in boasting and boasting is sin, then God commands us to sin when He commands our obedience for sanctification, for we will, by necessity boast in being made more holy (i.e. sanctified)! If we understand Paul to be rejecting good works in total because in doing them, they, by necessity, result in boasting and sin, then we cannot conclude otherwise. In other words, the faith alone view leads us straight into biblical incoherence, because everywhere in the Scriptures God commands our obedience, and never to we get a hint that this will by necessity lead us to sin, in fact just the opposite- His commands lead us away from sin. Paul's meaning comes into focus and maintains biblical coherence by understanding the limited and contextually defined purpose of Paul's argument.

Paul is arguing for faith in Jesus Christ for both Jew and Gentile, and against "works of the Mosaic law" which have been understood by Jews to be a legitimate cause of boasting before men and a claim against God by virtue of their flesh. The danger facing the church is not that false teachers are commanding men to obey God for justification, but that men are commanding circumcision which places confidence and boasting in the "flesh." This danger is articulated by Paul, "Not even those who are circumcised obey the law, yet they want you to be circumcised that they may boast about your flesh" (Gal.6:13). We must understand that Paul is not arguing against "works" as obedience to God through the commands of Jesus and the Apostles. To insist on this is to insist on much more than Paul ever meant to say in Romans 4:1-8.

Strong Tower #3

Christ is the end of the law so that there may be righteousness for everyone who believes. [For] Moses describes in this way the righteousness that is by law: "The man who does these things will live by them." But the righteousness that is by faith says, "Do not say in your heart, 'Who will ascend to heaven?' (That is to bring Christ down) or 'Who will descend into the deep?' (That is, to bring Christ up from the dead)." But what does it say? "The word is near you; it is in your mouth and in your heart," that is, the word of faith we are proclaiming: that if

135

you confess with your mouth, "Jesus is Lord," and believe in your heart that God raised him from the dead, you will be saved. For it is with your heart that you believe and are justified, and it is with your mouth that you confess and are saved. (Romans 10:4-9)

Once again, it is easy to understand the apparent value this passage would have for the faith alone teaching. Here Paul appears to place doing against believing as two antithetical ways of being justified before God. This antithesis is very similar to the one Paul sets up in our Galatians passage, since Paul again quotes Leviticus 18:5 and rejects doing the law and upholds faith as the way to be justified. The advocates of faith alone point out that Paul rejects the doing-way as "the righteousness that is by law" and upholds the faith-way as "the righteousness that is by faith." In what follows, Paul seems to emphasize the difference between faith and law by promoting "the word of faith we proclaim." This "word of faith" is interpreted to mean that if you simply confess your faith that Jesus is Lord, and believe in your heart that God raised him from the dead then the promise is yours. These teachers see this text as showing that a man is justified by faith alone, not by obedience as in the days of Moses.

First, all agree that Paul once again establishes an antithesis. But is he setting up a faith-way of relating to God over and against an obedience-way of relating to God? The passage itself argues against this kind of understanding. First, Paul asserts that the coming of Christ marks the "end of the law." He does not assert the end of obedience or of good works simply considered. Paul is arguing for the end of doing something *specific*, namely, "the law." Paul then gives reasons for the termination of the law. "For Moses describes in this way the righteousness that is by the law: 'The man who does these things will live by them'"(v.5). "The law" is forefront in Paul's mind, and it was by doing "the things" of the law that a person would be justified under the Old Covenant. He goes on, "But the righteousness that is by faith says: 'Do not say in your heart who will ascend into heaven? (That is to bring Christ down.)'" What is remarkable here is that Paul quotes Deuteronomy 30:12 to assert faith, which is from the law of Moses! Paul is using Moses' command to assert the necessity of faith, which is to say that Moses commanded the same thing in the law. What is Paul's point? His point is the same as Moses' in Deuteronomy 30. In

136

Deuteronomy 30, Moses was proclaiming that Israel need not go elsewhere to discover the will of God. They need not "go to heaven" or "descend into the deep." The will of God was not some deep mystery that needed to be discovered. "No, the word is very near you; it is in your mouth and in your heart so you may obey it" (30:14). The word at that time was the word of Moses. They need not go elsewhere, but rest content with God's provision in the law. Paul is now saying that the Word has come to us in human flesh. The will of God now is revealed not through the law, but through Jesus Christ. The antithesis Paul is setting up is not doing vs. believing, but the law vs. Jesus Christ who is "the end of the law." Notice the parallel:

"'No, the word is very near you; It is in your *mouth* and in your *heart*, so you may obey it' [Deut.30:14],

that is, the word of faith we are proclaiming:

That if you confess with your *mouth,* 'Jesus is Lord,' and believe in your *heart* that God raised him from the dead, you will be saved'" (Rom. 10:9).

The heart and mouth are to be involved in both covenants, but the focus is different. For Moses it was the word of the law, but for Paul and the New Covenant the focus is Christ who Himself is the living Word. The Word Himself has come down from heaven. We need not look past Him in order to discover God's will, and in this case, we need not look past Jesus and back to the law. Christ alone is all we need. This is the new word of faith.

The faith alone adherents will point out that Moses emphasized obeying while Paul was all about faith and believing. On the surface, this would appear to be the case. But we must look closer. The "word of faith" that Paul and the apostles are proclaiming, in contrast to Moses, is that "Jesus is Lord." Tightly connected to this confession is the belief that "God raised him from the dead." You must believe in Christ's resurrection from the dead in order to acknowledge Christ's present and very real lordship. This is where faith alone teachers run into trouble. What does it mean to "confess that Jesus is Lord?" Some hold that to confess that Jesus is Lord is to do just that, faith alone teaching renders a proper confession of Christ's lordship with our mouths as sufficient for justification. This is celebrated as a demonstration of the free grace of the gospel, that to merely confess Jesus is sufficient for salvation. But is this what Paul meant? It cannot be. How can Paul mean this when Jesus himself teaches the insufficiency of saying Jesus is Lord with our mouths yet not doing what he has said we are to do? "Not everyone who says to me, 'Lord, Lord' will enter the kingdom of heaven, but only he who does the will of my Father who is in heaven"(Mt.7:21).

For other faith alone teachers, it means that the fruit of faith is the confession that Jesus is Lord and that Paul places the fruit of faith (i.e. sanctification) prior to faith itself which alone justifies. So, according to them, in this verse Paul has justification and sanctification alongside one another. So to confess with your mouth is the sanctified fruit of faith, but to believe in your heart is all you have to do to be justified. However, how is it possible Paul can mean that confessing Jesus as our Lord has nothing to do with our justification when Paul himself holds out salvation as the promise for those who do? Salvation is made conditional not on just believing, but also upon confessing Christ's lordship (Rom.10:9,10). So if salvation is dependent upon confessing Christ as Lord, as Paul clearly asserts, and confessing Jesus as Lord entails more than saying Jesus is Lord with our mouths, as Jesus Himself asserts, then it follows quite reasonably that salvation is dependent upon doing what Jesus and His apostles have commanded us to do. To confess Jesus is Lord is to have Jesus Christ as our Lord, the Lord of our lives.

This makes good sense of our passage. In this passage Paul pits Moses in Leviticus 18:5 against Moses in Deuteronomy 30 in order to show that the faith Moses commanded for his people under the Old Covenant, that is, to believe the Word that he had given them in the law was sufficient for life, was the same kind of faith Paul and the apostles were requiring in response to Jesus. "The word of faith we are proclaiming" is different than the word of faith Moses proclaimed, but it is still a "word of faith." To live under Moses was to do the things Moses commanded to be done, things like circumcision and Sabbath-keeping. But the "word of faith" being proclaimed now is that "Jesus is Lord" as His resurrection from the dead has clearly demonstrated. With Jesus as Lord is a New Covenant, and with a New Covenant are things to be done just as Jesus has already said quite clearly, and nothing less than salvation is at stake in not only saying Jesus is Lord, but acknowledging Him as Lord in the biblical sense of the word.

At this point it is important that I acknowledge the possibility of the second faith alone understanding of Romans 10:9,10. It is possible that when Paul says, "For it is with your heart that you believe and are justified, and it is with your mouth that you confess and are saved" that Paul is talking about two aspects of our salvation. It is possible that Paul switches from justification, a momentary forensic declaration in the first clause, to the process of sanctification in the second clause and that Paul intends confessing Jesus and being saved as not referring to justification but to being made more holy through a sanctifying confession of Jesus. As a seminary professor of mine used to say, "All things are possible, but not all things are probable." I believe, while it is possible to see it this way, it is not at all likely this is how Paul intended to be understood. Let's look closer. The outline below shows Paul's logic in this text.

> "*If* you confess with your mouth 'Jesus is Lord'
> > *and*
> believe in your heart that Jesus rose from the dead,
> > *you will* be saved"(v.9).

As the above outline shows, the promise of being saved is dependent on meeting the twin conditions of confessing and believing. Confessing Jesus as Lord in the first clause and believing Jesus rose from the dead both lead to being saved. Then Paul makes an explanatory statement with the next verse:

> "*For* a man believes with his heart for justification
> > *and*
> confesses with his mouth for salvation" (v.10).

With this second phrase Paul is repeating himself. In verse 9, both confessing and believing lead to being saved. In verse 10, confessing leads to salvation and believing leads to justification. Either we believe Paul to mean, as he did in verse 9, that confessing and believing lead to the same thing—salvation, now in verse 10 described in two different ways, as justification and salvation, or we believe that Paul is speaking about two different movements in the process of salvation, namely, justification and sanctification. The first observation that makes the two movements view unlikely is the first phrase. If this were Paul's intention, it is odd that he would lump both confessing and believing as necessary for salvation and then in the next phrase make only confessing necessary for salvation and believing necessary for something different (justification). The second observation is that the proponents of faith alone make justification the first move in the process of salvation, with sanctification following in its wake. Why is it, then, that Paul mentions a sanctifying confession first and justifying belief second in verse 10, which is his explanatory clause? If this "process of salvation" were informing Paul's discourse then this is certainly odd. Calvin himself thinks so as he comments,

> The Word of the Lord ought to bring forth fruit wherever it exists, and our confession of the Word is the fruit of the mouth. To put confession before faith is an inversion of the order quite common in Scripture. The order would have been better if the faith of the heart had been put first, and the confession of the mouth, which arises from it, had followed."[46]

Notice, Calvin himself considers Paul to have "inverted the order" of salvation, and even finds it necessary to correct Paul in saying it "would have been better if the faith of the heart had been put first." If Calvin is right, then he is quite correct to conclude that Paul could have done a better job with it. But since Paul was not only a highly capable theologian in his own right, but as an apostle a teacher of theologians, and as a writer of Scripture, inspired by the Spirit of God, it is better to conclude that Paul did a fine job of explaining himself . It would be better to question our expectations of what Paul should have said. In conclusion, it is far more likely that Paul did not have this "order of salvation" in mind at all and that in this text justification and salvation are two different ways of describing the same reality, which is to be obtained by "confessing Jesus Christ as Lord."

That Paul intends Christ to be the focus, and faith in him—not faith as a unique New Covenant response is confirmed by what follows verse 10. See below:

> For it is with your heart that you believe and are justified, and it is with your mouth that you confess and are saved. For the

---

46 Calvin's commentary, 227.

Scripture says, "*Anyone* who trusts in him will never be put to shame." For there is *no difference between Jew and Gentile* - the same Lord is *Lord of all* and richly blesses *all* who call on him, for, "*everyone* who calls on the name of the Lord will be saved."

We can discern a tight logical progression in Paul's thought. Verses 11-13 establish the basis for verse 10. To paraphrase; "If you confess Jesus is Lord you will be saved, for 'anyone who trusts in the Lord will be saved.'" The tight logical progression makes Paul's focus very clear. Now in the New Covenant, "anyone," "everyone," "all" being saved is a new aspect of the New Covenant. Now "there is no difference between Jew and Gentile" even though there clearly was under the Old Covenant. Paul quotes Old Covenant prophets, Joel and Isaiah, who were prophesying a future time when God's message would be universal in its scope, when not just Israel will be summoned to "call upon the Lord," but every nation will hear the summons. Again, what is new about the New Covenant, is not trusting as a saving response, but the call for all to trust—Jew and Gentile alike. The stone that would cause men to stumble would not be the call to believe rather than obey, but it would be the call to faith in Jesus Christ as Lord of all mankind. This now pulls together this passage from where Paul began: "Christ is the end of the law so that there might be righteousness for everyone who believes....for there is no difference between Jew and Gentile—the same Lord is Lord of all and richly blesses all who call on him"(vv. 4, 12).

Conclusion

I have attempted in this appendix to explain three so-called strong tower passages of the faith alone view of our acceptance before God. I believe that I have demonstrated that these towers are not at all strong for faith alone, but rather, they point quite clearly to God's acceptance being based upon our allegiance to the Lord. To hold to the faith alone view leads to either explaining Paul incoherently and to accuse him of "inverting the order of salvation" or of the need to ignore the wider biblical context of Paul's thought. We cannot isolate particular sayings of any biblical writer in order to back our favorite doctrine. This is dishonest, and reveals a desire to not really hear Paul, but to hear our cherished traditions from his mouth. This must be combated with the utmost energy and forthrightness. May the Lord lead His church and the clear light of His truth.

www.ingramcontent.com/pod-product-compliance
Lightning Source LLC
Chambersburg PA
CBHW030005110426
42736CB00040BA/516